Amish Cooking

Wholesome and Simple Amish Recipe Cookbook

(Enjoy Easy and Homemade Amish Cooking With Delicious Amish Recipes)

Vernon Hester

Published By **Bella Frost**

Vernon Hester

All Rights Reserved

Amish Cooking: Wholesome and Simple Amish Recipe Cookbook (Enjoy Easy and Homemade Amish Cooking With Delicious Amish Recipes)

ISBN 978-1-7388580-7-1

No part of this guidebook shall be reproduced in any form without permission in writing from the publisher except in the case of brief quotations embodied in critical articles or reviews.

Legal & Disclaimer

The information contained in this book is not designed to replace or take the place of any form of medicine or professional medical advice. The information in this book has been provided for educational & entertainment purposes only.

The information contained in this book has been compiled from sources deemed reliable, and it is accurate to the best of the Author's knowledge; however, the Author cannot guarantee its accuracy and validity and cannot be held liable for any errors or omissions. Changes are periodically made to this book. You must consult your doctor or get professional medical advice before using any of the suggested remedies, techniques, or information in this book.

Upon using the information contained in this book, you agree to hold harmless the Author from and against any damages, costs, and expenses, including any legal fees potentially resulting from the application of any of the information provided by this guide. This disclaimer applies to any damages or injury caused by the use and application, whether directly or indirectly, of any advice or information presented, whether for breach of contract, tort, negligence, personal injury, criminal intent, or under any other cause of action.

You agree to accept all risks of using the information presented inside this book. You need to consult a professional medical practitioner in order to ensure you are both able and healthy enough to participate in this program.

Table Of Contents

Chapter 1: A Brief History Of Canning 1

Chapter 2: Starting Off 6

Chapter 3: Step-By-Step Guide To Water-Bath Canning.. 18

Chapter 4: Step-By-Step Guides To Pressure Canning 27

Chapter 5: An Important Note About Tattler Reusable Canning Lids 37

Chapter 6: Butters, Jams, And Jellies...... 46

Amish White Bread 148

Amish Baked Oatmeal......................... 150

Amish Soft Pretzels 152

Amish Turnips 155

Amish Meatloaf Recipe 157

Amish Noodles.................................... 159

Amish Apple Crisp 160

Amish Dip.. 162

Amish Friendship Bread And Starter 163

Amish Macaroni & Cheese 167

- Amish Baked Chicken 171
- Amish Pickled Eggs And Beets 173
- Dried Beef Gravy 174
- Amish Beef Stew 176
- Whole Wheat Bread 179
- Amish Crazy Quilt Pie 181
- Amish Baked Apples 183

Chapter 1: A Brief History Of Canning

When we take into account home canning, our minds proper now conjure up photos of orderly rows of jars filling pantry cabinets, appropriately loaded with meals and ready to be opened so we are able to create some of delectable food for our cherished ones. Summer gardens produce lots of food for numerous delicious feasts at some stage in the cruel wintry climate months. Let the wintry weather storms come—we are capable of rest assured that our own family might be well fed because of the truth our pantry shelves are stocked with a flavor of summer season's bounty.

Canning our food can also moreover appear to be the embodiment of the hardworking homemaker, however canning did no longer originate as a desire to the housewife's dinnertime predicament. Instead, canning superior as a reaction to a question raised by using the use of war. In the past due 1700s, Emperor Napoleon Bonaparte of France have become concerned that his soldiers had been now not very well nourished when they went a long way from domestic. He understood that they required a reliable technique for retaining meals stable to consume for prolonged intervals. As a cease end result, he furnished a monetary prize to the individual that can also want to plot a dependable approach for food protection.

Nicolas Appert, a French confectionery maker, brewer, distiller, and chef, steps in. Appert located that the use of heat to meals in sealed glass bottles maintained the food. The French army efficaciously experimented with warmth-preserved meals on extended journeys inside the early 1800s. They fed on canned meat, greens, fruit, and milk. However, it'd take extra than 50 years to find out why the canning method succeeded. Finally, Louis Pasteur proved that the improvement of microbes motives meals spoiling and that sealing meals into jars or cans with excessive heat kills those bacteria, making canned meals steady to eat months, if not years, later.

Several years after Appert's discovery, an Englishman named Peter Durand placed a manner to well seal food in tin-included iron cans. The first industrial canning plant in England grow to be created in 1813. Even in spite of the truth that those meals cans were particularly high-priced and required a chisel and hammer to open, the food canning organisation turn out to be born. The navy and explorers mainly implemented canned food, and it wasn't until the Nineteen Twenties that home canning became famous among homemakers.

In 1858, a tinsmith in Philadelphia called John Mason invented a glass "fruit jar" with threads on the jar's pinnacle and matching threads on a metallic band glued down on top of a zinc cowl with a rubber gasket. The canning jar technique have become easy and plenty less steeply-priced to low-earnings human beings for the primary time. The Lightning jar modified into invented in 1882. These jars featured glass lids held in region thru steel clamps and a rubber gasket. Atlas jars additionally carried out this approach. Until the Sixties, the Lightning-type jar system emerge as made inside the United States, and European agencies persevered to supply similar pots (Weck and Leifheit are such companies). They are lovable jars which may be to be had in loads of forms and sizes.

Meanwhile, in the United States, Ball jars (1886) and Kerr jars (1903) have been delivered with the two-piece jewelry and lids that we're acquainted with nowadays. The metallic lid had a totally associated gasket that sealed the contents in the jars. The groups in the long run merged, and the Jarden Corporation now makes and distributes Ball, Kerr, Bernardin (particularly in Canada), and Golden Harvest jars.

Another crucial soar forward came in 1976 on the equal time as Stieg Tattler reusable lids were delivered to the marketplace. During the Nineteen Sixties and 1970s, at the peak of the "again to the land" movement, there was this type of growth in interest in domestic canning that jars and lids were regularly in quick deliver, and the appearance of Tattler reusable have become a proper away cease end result of this scarcity. Tattler lids are made out of a thick, BPA-loose plastic composite. A reusable rubber ring or gasket creates the seal. Tattler lids and rubber rings have been confirmed to go through a long time or more, and the rubber rings are every so often the brilliant replacements required after a few years of usage.

Even despite the fact that the canning approach has modified little in the previous centuries, research and experiments performed with the resource of universities and authorities organizations have perfected the safety necessities for individual objects being preserved, which may be usually up to date as wanted. So, even if you have a recipe surpassed down from the only which you love grandma or aunt, it's far main to rely upon the most updated statistics. You may probable still use your preceding favored recipe, however the processing time or manner also can need to be adjusted. You'd be realistic to accomplish that during your circle of relatives's protection.

Chapter 2: Starting Off

Over the years, I've met many humans, specifically ladies, who want to learn how to can food however are worried about doing it securely. I need to provide you the assure that it isn't complicated or perhaps mysterious, however as an alternative a rely of following and in line with instructions. If we aggregate up a recipe or experiment with additives at the same time as cooking or baking for our family and pals, we may additionally turn out to be with a few element that tastes horrific however does no longer make our loved ones ill. However, following set up protocols is needed in canning—this is not the area to experiment! That's now not to say you can not "create" your recipe; you without a doubt can, however you will want to get cushty with the device and educate yourself at the way to make adjustments wisely first.

There are number one processes of canning: boiling water-bath canning and stress canning. And there are basically types of elements: excessive-acid meals with a pH of four.6 or under and espresso-acid (alkaline) meals with a pH more than four.6. High-acid elements are regularly water-bathed, however low-acid meals require stress canning at temperatures better than boiling to be steady.

The following is a top stage view of each method's device, however in the following chapters, I'll go into greater detail, with real, step-through-step commands that you could observe while you're canning.

Boiling Water-Bath Canners

High-acid materials may be canned in boiling water baths, together with jams, jam pastes, jam butter, jam preserves, jam marmalade, fruit juice, fruit pie filling, tomatoes, tomato sauce, and tomato juice. (lemon juice or a few other acidifier is introduced to tomato merchandise to ensure that the acid degree is excessive sufficient to securely can the ones foods the use of the boiling water-bathtub technique); and pickles and relishes are canned the usage of the boiling water-bathtub approach.

Any big pot with an top notch-turning into lid can suffice. Still, water-tub canners explicitly designed for canning ingredients are cheap and punctiliously proportioned, making the minor funding properly clearly clearly worth it. You'll want a bottom rack to maintain the jars off the pot's ground, and the pool need to be tall enough simply so the jars are covered with the resource of two inches of water with 1 to 2 inches of air location above that. If your pressure canner is tall enough, you could furthermore use it for water-bath canning.

After getting geared up the meals for canning, fill the jars midway with the food or liquid, screw at the lids and jewelry, and region them in the canner, crammed midway with boiling water. Once all your jars are in feature, upload greater boiling water to cowl them through using inches. Cover the canner and warmth it till the water reaches 212°F (one hundred°C). After getting a rolling boil, you'll start the processing time, that could variety from 5 minutes to 112 hours. You can lessen the warm temperature slightly all through the processing time, but ensure the water by no means stops boiling.

The oxygen is removed from the jars by way of boiling them in water. This aids in forming an excellent seal and is good sufficient to kill the mildew, yeast, and bacterial organisms inside the meal. Even despite the fact that boiling at 212° won't kill clostridium botulinum spores—which reason botulism, a doubtlessly lethal toxin—immoderate acid levels in elements with pH 4.6 or decrease prevent their increase. As a end result, canned food is stable to consume.

Before taking the plunge into stress canning, many people decide on water-tub canning to "take a look at the waters." Although that is sincerely a rely of desire (or courage!), strain canning is in addition clean. Green beans are some of the most reachable meals to hold thru pressure canning.

Canners under Pressure

Vegetables, meat, fowl, fish, seafood, and mixture recipes the usage of low-acid objects must be pressure canned at temperatures extra than 212°F (a hundred°C). This is because of the reality the pH degree in those low-acid meals is truly too immoderate to inhibit the formation of Clostridium botulinum, the micro organism that motives botulism. When the spores are in an anaerobic environment (missing oxygen, as in canned food jars), they might growth and create lethal portions of botulinum toxin. As a stop end result, pressure is needed to elevate the temperature, which strain canning does thru elevating the temperature within the subject to 240°F. Botulinum spores are destroyed at the same time as canned food is processed effectively for appropriate lengths of time, and the canned food is solid to maintain and in the end devour.

Unlike a water-bathtub canner, you could need to buy a strain canner. While a pressure canner does not come reasonably-priced, it's far an funding as a way to final you for many years if well maintained. Pressure canners are classified into sorts: folks who hire a gasket to shut and seal the lids when they had been locked into region (which include the Presto brand), and those which may be "gasket much much less" and seal via the usage of using heavy-responsibility screws that tighten the locked lid to the canner's body (along with the

All American). Gasket canners generally are a outstanding deal plenty much less luxurious than gasket-a whole lot a lot much less canners, but you will want to alternate the gaskets every 12 months or so, relying on how regularly you use them. Gaskets are an entire lot an awful lot much less than ten bucks, so that is a bit of extra investment, and with the coins you saved on the acquisition charge as compared to the gasket, you will be beforehand even after a few years of utilization.

Pressure canners are also organized with a dial or weighted gauge that displays while the critical stress (psi or pounds consistent with rectangular inch) in the canner has been attained. Dial gauges should be monitored sooner or later of meals processing to make sure that the psi does not move beneath the advocated diploma. In addition, you need to affirm your dial gauge as speedy as a 365 days to ensure that it nevertheless offers an correct analyzing. Weighted gauges, instead, exhaust small amounts of steam all through the complete processing duration, causing the weighted gauge to rock back and forth, so you may not want to test the gauge visually constantly — as an opportunity, you will be capable of recognize that the stress is at the perfect psi surely via the use of paying attention to the rocking of the gauge, allowing you to move around greater in preference to being caught near the stove for long intervals as even as the use of a dial gauge. Another benefit of the weighted gauge approach is that it does now not need to be examined every yr until damaged.

Another item to mention about weighted gauges: they regularly consist of a one-piece gauge this is weighted at 15 psi, however you can get a 3-piece gauge that adjusts to 5, 10, or 15 psi. These three-piece gauges are the precise to use and allow the most flexibility of motion during processing considering the fact that, if you are processing at ten psi, you can concentrate the rocking and recognize that the whole lot is OK with out looking.

Other Equipment Required

You may require a few extra materials to well can.

Jars for Canning: There are diverse dimensions and shapes of canning jars available, beginning from 4 oz.. To a 1/2 of-gallon, however the most famous sizes are half of of-pints, pints, and quarts. The half of of-gallon measures have to amazing be used for apple or grape juice, but they make excellent garage jars for sugar, beans, oats, and other dry gadgets. No depend how lots the jar holds, the apertures are both large or massive-mouth. Only use canning jars thinking about that they've been successfully tempered, and breakage inside the canner is decreased to a minimum. Mayonnaise or empty meals jars are not appropriate substitutes for commercially synthetic canning jars. (Although some individuals declare to have used recycled mayonnaise jars efficaciously, it isn't always recommended.)

Lids: The maximum popular lids are made from elements: a steel lid with a hoop of sealing compound spherical the threshold and a screw band that holds the lid in place for processing. Reusable lids (Tattlers by way of using Stieg) function further to the 2-piece lids however are recommended to final two a long time. The reusable are greater high-priced on the start, but if you can food regularly, they will more than pay for themselves over the years. There are greater jars with unusual sizes and lid systems, however those are uncommon in maximum shops and have to be sold online. Still, a few are lovely—if high priced—and may be ideal for a completely precise domestic-canned present or your chosen recipe.

The lids are to be had in considerable or large-mouth sizes to suit the everyday or big-mouth canning jars. You can not trade them; you need to have an appropriate period, depending on your pot. You will want drastically extra lids than screw bands (except you use Tattler reusable) thinking about the reality that covers need to fine be used as soon as, but screw bands may be used time and again till they rust or get damaged.

Removes air bubbles: You can use a plastic (no steel!) knife such as you'll cope with a picnic, however you may moreover buy a bubble remover/headspace measurer that works in fact as nicely. This beneficial device has graded notches that show fill traces from ¼ to one inch on one end and is tapered to slip over the insides of the jars to take away bubbles before setting the lid on.

Funnel: A funnel fits into the jars and makes filling them tidy and easy. Horns are especially handy for loading warm meals or liquid into jars. Canning funnels are designed to in shape significant-mouth and regular-mouth pots; certainly one is needed.

Jar lifters: Jar lifters are accessible for moving complete jars into and out of the canner with out being burned. They resemble big tongs with rubber handles that firmly preserve jars at the identical time as transferring them. A jar lifter is crucial, for my part.

Tongs or a magnetic lid lifter: Magnetic lid lifters are pencil-standard gear with a magnet on one give up that dispose of warm water lids. Tongs for canning are specially built and are longer than what is normally furnished within the kitchen device class. They're available everywhere canning substances are bought.

A small pocket book: It's a great concept to maintain a document of everything you hold. Date, amount of food collected (in pounds, quarts, and so forth.), variety (in the case of fruits and greens), recipe applied, and amount and duration of jars yielded are all valuable facts. This form of records may be quite useful within the future at the same time as choosing how a exquisite deal of whatever to can for the subsequent 12 months. Furthermore, analyzing thru your canning "diary" and remembering what you have preserved at some point of the years is incredibly fun. This is the spot to put in writing any notes or charming data you need to don't forget.

Of route, there are numerous unique system to be had that will help you in conjunction with your canning obligations. Juicers, strainers, cherry pitters, slicers, and food mills are to be had counting on the gadgets you need to approach. And at the same time as those system also can make your challenge much much less complex and faster, they will be not required to do it. However, if you want canning, you'll most possibly gather those treasured gadgets over the years. I agree with they are properly certainly well worth every penny I've spent gathering my collection of accessible gadgets through the years.

Chapter 3: Step-By-Step Guide To Water-Bath Canning

Processing timeframes will range primarily based on the type of meals you are canning, but the actions you follow to ensure stable processing will continuously be comparable. And, irrespective of how a wonderful deal you exercise canning, having those instructions to be had will guarantee that you do not neglect a critical step and become with incorrectly canned food or jars that do not seal.

1. Inspect your canner to ensure that each one elements are in excellent strolling order: The canner basis want to be freed from dents and warping. Purchase a alternative rack if the best that holds the general jars has deteriorated from preceding use. (You do not want it to fail on the equal time as lifting a massive load of warm pots.) Clean the canner and lid.

2. Examine and clean your jars, lids, and screw bands: Check for chipped or fractured pots, an entire ring of sealing compound spherical the brink of the covers, and twisted or rusted bands. Wash jars with warmth soapy water or

run them through a everyday cycle in your dishwasher, leaving the pots unopened till ready to use. If hand cleaning, rinse the jars after washing them and set them in a saucepan with sufficient water to cowl them. Ensure they will be soaked in water until you're geared up to apply them. Alternatively, set your jars on a baking sheet and bake them at a hundred seventy five°F until needed.

Lids ought to be wiped clean in heat soapy water, rinsed, and positioned in each other pot with enough water to cowl them. Simmer the lids in water, but do no longer permit the water to boil considering this could damage the sealing compound and purpose a seal failure. You actually need to look little bubbles in the pot.

Wash the bands in heat soapy water, then rinse and dry them in advance than storing them till required. Alternatively, you can area the rounds in the pot of water with the lids already nestled in them, equipped to be lifted out on the equal time as sealing the food jars.

three. Preheat the canner: Fill your water-bathtub canner halfway with water, set it for your big burner, and heat till the water is heat however not boiling. Insert the canner rack into the canner or region the rack handles on the canner's top area when you have that shape of rack (most water-bathtub canners include a stand protected).

4. Fill the jars: Fill every jar one at a time. Fill the pot with the additives listed beneath and lid it in advance than taking place to the subsequent jar and continuing the way: a. Fill the jar midway with meals and any liquid. Pack the jars tightly however do not squish the meals.

b. Determine headspace. The hole among the jar's top rim and the pinnacle of the meals or liquid is referred to as headspace. In preferred, 1 inch of headspace is wanted for low-acid meals (meat, vegetables, hen, legumes, and fish); 12 inches of headspace is needed for excessive-acid elements which incorporates tomatoes and fruits; and 18-14 inches of headspace is wanted for juices, jams, jellies, and pickles.

c. Remove any air bubbles. Run a plastic knife or an air bubble tool at some stage in the jar's elements to cast off bubbles. Regardless of whether you accept as true with you studied there aren't any air bubbles, avoid skipping this step. Don't panic if you overlook this step—your food will although be steady, no matter the fact that now and again bubbles can reason jars to not close. I'll insert the knife alongside the jar's thing and gently press it toward the center. I do nicely to replicate this method 3 or four instances, setting the knife in a specific vicinity whenever.

d. Clean the jar rims. Cleaning the rims of jars is straightforward with a wet paper towel. Wrap a moist paper towel or washcloth throughout the jar's rim. Make superb there aren't any fragments of meals or spices clinging to the pinnacle vicinity due to the fact the sealing compound wishes to be in touch with the jar top all the manner round for the jar to close efficiently.

e. Attach lids and bands. Screw on the bar after putting the pinnacle at the jar, sealing the side down, so it is in touch with the jar rim. Screw it on snugly however no longer too tightly—no, you want to crank down as hard as viable. The tightness guideline is sometimes phrased as "finger-tip tight."

Note approximately Tattlers: If you are the use of Tattlers, see Chapter 5 for commands on a manner to screw on the Tattler plastic lids—it is slightly awesome from the greater popular -piece approach.

f. Place the filled jar in the canner rack. Place your sealed pot into the canner's body, using the jar lifter to keep away from burning yourself. Remember to balance the jars via positioning them contrary a in addition in area of aspect by manner of aspect, which may additionally moreover motive the rack to topple. I commonly begin through placing the primary jar within the middle function of the canner rack because it seems to help stability out the load as I maintain to add jars.

5. Get the canner prepared for processing: Lower the rack with the filled jars into the canner after your big load is in region. (This diploma also can additionally want the usage of heated pads.) Add simmering water to cover the jars via 1-2 inches if critical. Turn the warmth as a lot as medium-excessive,

cover the canner, and produce the water to a whole boil.

6. Altitude processing and adjustment: Set the recipe processing time timer after the canner water has reached a complete rolling boil. However, relying at the altitude you're living in, you may need to alternate the processing durations. The following are the increased processing instances:

Altitude in Feet	Increased Processing Time
0 – 1,000	No adjustment in minutes
1,001 – 3,000	5 minutes
3,001 – 6,000	10 minutes
6,001 – 8,000	15 minutes
8,001 – 10,000	20 minutes

You also can get your altitude via touring to www.Earthtools.Org and entering into your location anywhere within the international.

The water should in no way prevent boiling inside the route of this processing period. Also, the boiling water degree need to in no way move below the tops of the lids; you may add boiling water if required to keep the jars properly blanketed. When the processing time is over, remove the canner lid and flip off the warmth. (Remember to place on warm gloves and open the lid to direct the steam a long way from you.) Allow the jars to live within the canner for five minutes before casting off them. Place the jars on a dry fabric or wooden lowering board with air place among them and leave them to sit back completely. Do not press down at the lid's center or tighten the bands.

Tattlers: When using Tattler reusable lids, steady the screw bands right away after getting rid of the jars from the canner. Because the contents are quite warm, placed on oven mitts. Crank the screw bands as difficult as you can.

7. Examine the jars for suitable seals: When the little dome element inside the middle of the lid drops down, you understand the jars are sealed. This can appear with a loud popping bang (that is quite enjoyable!), or it could take area often, but as quickly as the dome is added down, the jar is close. If the crown within the middle of a lid stays up after

severa hours (indicating that the jar hasn't sealed), location the pot within the refrigerator and employ the food indoors some days. You also can reprocess the meals with a ultra-modern cover and processing time.

Check every jar after about 12 hours to ensure it has a very good seal: Remove the bands and squeeze the lid to make certain that the center is tight and concave (curved slightly downward). Lift the jar carefully by way of the usage of the lid's thing collectively collectively together with your fingertips. The cowl need to be solid. After that, easy the pots with a wet towel. Attach a label or write the contents of the jar at the lid. It's moreover a incredible concept to encompass the date so that you may additionally eat the older jars first.

Note approximately using Tattlers: Because Tattler lids are constructed of hard plastic, they will now not pop down, and consequently there may be no visible proof that a seal has been regular. After round 12 hours, or while the meals jar has completely cooled, get rid of the screw band and carefully enhance the jar thru the rim to check for a terrific seal. You need if you want to deliver the pot with the aid of the plastic seal with out it falling off if the seal has been created.

8. Clean your canner and device: earlier than the use of them all over again. Before sealing and storing the canner, ensure the whole thing is dehydrated.

Chapter 4: Step-By-Step Guides To Pressure Canning

Processing timeframes will range primarily based definitely on the sort of food you're canning, but the actions you have a look at to make certain stable processing will constantly be the equal. And, irrespective of how lots you could or how extended you have got been doing it, having those instructions inside the front of you whenever will guarantee that you don't forget approximately a important step and chance incorrectly canned meals or jars that fail to seal. This is mainly vital at the same time as canning below pressure.

1. Inspect your canner to make certain that all factors are in exceptional running order: The canner foundation ought to be free of dents and warping. Purchase a replacement rack if the handiest that lies on the lowest of the pressure canner has deteriorated from preceding use. Clean the canner and lid. Check that the gasket underneath the lid's aspect stays comfortable and hasn't dried out or damaged. To make sure that the vent pipe on the top is plain, insert a toothpick or pipe cleaner thru it. To make sure that the vent is

plain, keep the lid as a lot because the moderate and leaf through the vent pipe—there ought to be a hint hollow seen. Your canner's manual may additionally provide inspection hints, and in case you discover that you require new components, do not use your canner till you've got modified them.

2. Examine and easy your jars, lids, and screw bands: Check for chipped or fractured pots, a whole ring of sealing compound around the threshold of the covers, and twisted or rusted bands. Wash the jars with hot soapy water, or run a ordinary cycle for your dishwasher, leaving the pots unopened till prepared to apply. If hand cleansing, rinse the jars after washing them and set them in a saucepan with enough water to cover them. Have them soaked in water till you're ready to use them. Alternatively, set your jars on a baking sheet and bake them at 100 75°F till wanted.

Lids must be wiped easy in warmness soapy water, rinsed, and positioned in every different pot with enough water to cowl them. Simmer the tops as properly, however do not allow the water to boil because this could harm the sealing compound and cause a seal failure.

Wash and dry the bands before the usage of them, or location them in the pot of water with the lids.

three. Preheat the canner: Fill your pressure canner to approximately three inches deep with water after putting the canner rack into the bottom (somewhere round 3 to 4 quarts commonly suffices, counting on the dimensions of your canner). Place the canner on your maximum effective burner. Make the water warm however not boiling.

4. Fill the jars: Fill every jar separately. Fill the pot with the materials indexed under and lid it in advance than taking place to the subsequent jar and persevering with the tool:
a. Fill the jar halfway with meals and any liquid. Pack the jars tightly however do not squish the meals.

b. Determine headspace. The hole most of the jar's top rim and the top of the meals or liquid is called headspace. In fashionable, 1 inch of headspace is wanted for low-acid meals (meat, vegetables, chicken, legumes, and fish); 12 inches of headspace is wanted for excessive-acid components together with tomatoes and end result; and 18-14 inches of headspace is wanted for juices, jams, jellies, and pickles. c. Remove any air bubbles. Run a plastic knife or an air bubble device throughout the jar's additives to eliminate bubbles. Avoid skipping this step even if you accept as authentic with there aren't any air bubbles present. If you pass this step, your food will although be stable, however every now and then bubbles can also moreover motive jars not to close or, worse, to interrupt in the canner, leaving you with a multitude. I'll insert the knife along the jar's component and lightly press it toward the middle. I make sure to copy this technique three or four instances, putting the knife in a excellent location every time.

d. Clean the jar rims. Cleaning the rims of jars is easy with a moist paper towel. Wrap a wet paper towel or washcloth across the jar's rim. Make positive there aren't any fragments of meals or spices clinging to the top thing for the motive that sealing compound need to be in contact with the jar pinnacle all of the way round for the jar to shut efficaciously.

e. Attach lids and bands. Screw on the bar after placing the pinnacle on the jar, sealing the side down, so it's far in touch with the jar rim. Screw it on snugly however now not too tightly—no, you want to crank down as tough as viable. The tightness tenet is every now and then phrased as "finger-tip tight." Note approximately Tattlers: If you're the usage of Tattlers, see Chapter five for commands on a manner to screw at the Tattler plastic lids—slightly one in every of a kind from the greater famous -piece technique.

f. Place the crammed jar inside the canner rack. Place your sealed jar into the canner's body, the use of the jar lifter to keep away from burning your self. Remember to balance the pots via the usage of positioning them opposite every other in preference to facet through the use of thing, that could likely motive the rack to topple. I usually start with the useful resource of way of putting the primary jar inside the center characteristic of the canner rack as it appears to assist balance out the weight as I maintain to feature jars.

five. Get the canner prepared for processing: Lower the rack with the filled jars into the canner after your entire load is in place. (This diploma can also want using heated pads.) Add simmering water to cowl the jars through 1-2 inches if vital. Turn the warmth as much as medium-excessive, cover the canner, and bring the water to a complete boil. Do no longer yet positioned the strain regulator at the vent pipe!

6. Remove the air from the canner. Heat the canner and contents till a non-prevent pass of steam exits from the lid's vent pipe. Although you can not normally see the steam exiting, you can listen and experience it. But be cautious! You will burn your hand if you positioned it too near the escaping steam. Allow 7 to 10 mins for the steam to break out via the vent pipe. It's OK to reveal down the warm temperature for 10 minutes, however make certain the moisture maintains venting.

7. Connect the strain regulator to the vent pipe. After you have got installation the strain

regulator on the vent pipe, you could crank up the warm temperature. As stress will increase in the canner, the pointer at the gauge will start to drift. When the stress registers the proper psi, reduce the warm temperature as follows to hold the precise pressure:

Altitude in Feet	Weighted Gauge	Dial Gauge
0 – 1,000	10	11
1,001 – 2,000	15	11
2,001 – 4,000	15	12
4,001 – 6,000	15	13
6,001 – 8,000	15	14
8,001 – 10,000	15	15

Note: You also can furthermore locate your altitude by way of manner of touring www.Earthtools.Org and getting into your place everywhere around the sector.

8. Processing. Set your timer in step with the recipe pointers after the proper pressure. Check your gauge regularly to make sure the pressure in no way falls underneath the right psi. If this takes place, you will must restart the timer. Once the pressure has reached the popular diploma, reduce the warmth barely to keep the psi. Instead of turning the burner

down, make minor adjustments to study what takes vicinity to the strain.

9. The cooling segment. When the processing time is over, cast off the pressure canner from the heat and place it on any other burner to kick back. Remove the weighted gauge from the vent pipe, and do no longer cast off the quilt! Allow the stress within the canner to surely cross once more to zero. Wait each different 5 minutes before removing the weighted gauge and carefully casting off the lid, making sure to elevate it truely so the steam exits a long way from your face. Use oven mitts and keep with caution.

10. Remove the jars from the canner. Place the jars on a material or wood lowering board, spaced approximately an inch aside, with oven mitts and your jar lifter to allow air to drift spherical them. Don't overtighten the bands. Allow the jars to relax absolutely till they acquire room temperature.

Note approximately Tattlers: When the usage of Tattler reusable lids, secure the screw bands proper away after removing the jars from the canner. Because the contents are pretty heat, placed on oven mitts. Crank the screw bands difficult.

eleven. Inspect the jars for ok seal. When the little dome component within the middle of the lid drops down, you recognize the jars are sealed. This can also appear rapid with a noisy popping sound (this is particularly enjoyable!), or it can take a chunk longer, however as soon as the dome is introduced down, the jar is sealed. If the crown in the center of a lid remains up after severa hours (indicating that the pot hasn't closed), vicinity the jar inside the fridge and make use of the food inner some days. You may reprocess the meals with a present day cowl.

12. Check each jar after about 12 hours to make certain it has an first-rate seal: Remove the bands and squeeze the lid to make sure that the middle is tight and concave (curved slightly downward). Lift the jar carefully with the useful resource of the lid's side together with your fingertips. The cowl have to be constant. After that, easy the pots with a moist towel. Attach a label or write the contents of the jar at the lid. It's additionally

an notable concept to embody the date so you may additionally eat the older jars first.

Note regarding using Tattlers: Because Tattler lids are built of hard plastic, they'll not pop down; therefore, there may be no obvious evidence that a seal has been installed. After round 12 hours, or while the food jar has virtually cooled, do away with the screw band and punctiliously increase the pot with the aid of the rim to check for an incredible seal. You must be capable of deliver the jar with the aid of manner of the plastic seal without it falling off if the seal has been created.

Chapter 5: An Important Note About Tattler Reusable Canning Lids

Tattler reusable canning lids and rubber earrings may be used for almost 20 years earlier than the rubber jewelry want to get replaced—and the meals-steady plastic lids can remaining lots longer. They may be used for water-bathtub or pressure canning and are in particular appropriate for immoderate-acid food like pickles for the cause that rigid plastic lids will no longer rust through the years.

The white plastic lids are thicker than elegant two-piece lids, and the gaskets are distinctly skinny and slim. Use a traditional screw band just like those with Ball and Kerr jars to place the covers for your canning jars. (These are to be had one after the opposite anywhere canning substances are presented.)

When the usage of Tattlers, there can be no obvious sign that a seal has been fashioned till you cast off the screw band and raise the jar to decide if the seal end up created. This way that the meals stays inside the pots until absolutely bloodless, irrespective of whether a seal has been fashioned. This want to now not be a huge deal, however in case you discover that a jar hasn't been properly sealed, right away refrigerate the contents, reprocess it, or devour it.

My Individual Learning Experience Making Use of Tattlers

When I first discovered about Tattler reusable lids, I have become intrigued—the idea of in no manner having to repurchase lids appealed to me due to the reality I can locate masses of jars of food each 365 days. It failed to take a whole lot arithmetic to decide out that the use of them could likely keep me money within the long time. So I went out and were given numerous containers of lids and gaskets and commenced out experimenting.

My canning undertaking at the day I first used Tattlers grow to be ground red meat. I can get plenty of meat due to the fact I like having geared up-made meal objects available for the ones instances as soon as I'm in a hurry to get dinner on the desk or once I'm weary and need my version of "rapid meals." But, no longer like culmination and vegetables, meat is some thing I no longer make for myself—I need to spend a part of my hard-earned cash to buy the meats that I eat.

Another detail to say at this factor, I've been canning—a number of canning—for forty years and feature come to be a hold close food preserver 15 years inside the beyond. I'm a canning professional. So I believed I'd haven't any problem managing Tattlers.

How was I incorrect?

I filled 9-pint jars with ground beef and then screwed at the Tattlers consistent with the bundle deal specifications, which said, "Screw band on jar loosely." Hold the lid at the identical time as tightening the metallic screw band collectively with your fingertip. Avoid overtightening. During processing, the product should be allowed to vent."

When I first study the instructions, I perception they have been easy, however I right away determined that "finger-tip tight" became a relative term. What precisely does "finger-tip tight" suggest, I wondered? I installed the lids, placed the jars in my stress canner, and processed them. I emerge as giddy about all the coins I anticipated to keep over the subsequent decades.

The processing has completed. Screw bands had been right away tightened as directed. The cooling time is over. The fun element modified into now—casting off the screw bands and attempting out for a seal. It never befell to me that I may also come across any problems. Yet I did. I had a pretty higher than 40% failure fee. That way 4 of my nine jars are not sealing. I emerge as stunned and more than a piece annoyed.

So I did a few greater research. I contacted Tattler's useful personnel and check blog entries regarding particular people's critiques online. I selected to use Tattlers again after receiving masses of feedback. But for the subsequent hundreds, I used Tattlers for 1/2 of the burden and the 2-piece earrings and seals for the alternative half of of. I had achievement, and I'm beginning to respect reusable.

Success Hints

You'll every be making use of Tattlers proper or incorrectly. And there can be a studying curve, so do not be discouraged if you have sealing screw ups on the begin, as I did. Continue to alter your technique until you find what works wonderful to your canning technique. The maximum hard a part of canning the use of Tattlers seems to be tightening the lids at the jars earlier than processing. Thus this is the step you want to reflect onconsideration on and tweak particularly if you have problems. To help you in records this step, underneath are severa techniques to offer an explanation for the same element: the manner to successfully tighten the band to installation a seal on the identical time as the use of a Tattler:

• Place the lid on the jar and keep it together with your finger whilst finger-tip tightening the metal screw band. Don't overtighten for the reason that food in the pot desires to vent at some level in the cooking segment.

• Screw the lid and screw band onto the jar precisely like you will a trendy -piece lid. Then take a step lower back and remove the screw band approximately 1 / 4-inch to allow the food to vent in some unspecified time in the future of processing.

• Place the lid and screw band at the jar, and tighten the band without a doubt till the grooves seize on the jar's ridges. Screw on loosely because the food desires to respire at the equal time as processing.

Hopefully, this sort of descriptions will resonate with you, and additionally you may not have a tough begin as I had.

You may additionally try canning half of of of your load with Tattlers and half of with regular -piece lids and bands until you're snug with them. That manner, if a seal fails at the same time as studying, you may not have to devour severa jars of available food in a rush.

You can also strive out Tattlers by using way of filling them with water and canning some trial hundreds to peer how a success you are. You won't waste food if the jars do not seal well. Continue until you've got got were given released 3 full canner hundreds with all of the jars stuffed.

Lid Removal:

When commencing jars of food can with the equal antique two-piece earrings and seals, without a doubt take hold of a bottle opener and pa the lid off the pot. But with Tattlers, you will want to do subjects a bit in a one-of-a-kind manner.

You ought to be careful at the same time as taking off your jars due to the reality you want to hold and reuse the plastic lids and gaskets. Tattler explains the gadget: "When removing the lid, lightly placed a table knife among the rubber and the jar to loosen the seal—do not use a pointy knife."

I attempted it, and it wasn't easy because of the fact I couldn't get an super grip maximum of the lid and the seal—there may be not enough location. When I ultimately opened the pinnacle, the contents inside the jar spilled out. I attempted the usage of a bottle opener to open the pot, which labored, but I changed into traumatic about the use of a semi-sharp metal device due to Tattler's advice to "do not use a pointy knife." So I went to the store to buy a plastic bottle opener that became touted as suitable for humans with hand arthritis. It is broader and thicker than its metallic counterpart and is composed of thick plastic in area of metallic. It moreover abilties a plastic pry region, which I believed might also help me open my jars with out breaking or warping the plastic lids or destructive the gasket. So some distance, so proper—it appears to function efficaciously, and I want to keep using it.

So, ought to you do not forget Tattler reusable lids? They have an area within the canning kitchen, in my opinion. You may additionally moreover buy a huge amount and then use it again, that may be a large gain. Your fee variety may be impacted in reality as quickly as, and you may constantly have your substances on hand—no greater last-minute trips to the store to buy greater lids even as you run out. Being prepared is mostly a right element. Tattlers are some thing I use.

But I moreover keep an intensive inventory of Ball and Kerr -piece lids and bands to be had, which I use regularly. I like them due to the fact that they may be easy and with out issues available in most locations. Experiment and phrase whether or not or not Tattlers have an area in your kitchen. You could be happy with the very last outcomes.

RECIPES

Chapter 6: Butters, Jams, And Jellies

Amish women can get numerous jars of butter, jams, jellies, and preserves sooner or later of harvest. Fruit is most customarily grown on their belongings, and preserving the abundance in season makes genuine experience. When the wintry climate snow flies, those jars of jellied goodness will beautify many a meal, and families will pleasure within the lingering taste of summer season.

In days lengthy gone via using, earlier than commercially packaged pectin have become available, jellied food modified into made by using manner of the usage of extracting the juice or crushing the fruit after which consisting of sugar and cooking the syrup down until it have become completed. But consequences may also need to differ extensively: the riper the fruit used, the a lot a good deal less pectin changed into gift, and overcooking (clean to do) supposed that the jam or jelly tasted burnt. And from time to time, a farmwife may probable overcook her fruit and emerge as with syrup in area of jam or jelly with out this means that that to. You can despite the fact that make jams and jellies this manner, but the use of packaged pectin is greater doable—the machine doesn't take as lengthy and your results, every so often sudden, are an lousy lot higher. (I'll inform you the way to apply the lengthy-put together dinner, no delivered pectin technique in the Jams and Jellies sections under.)

Butters

Fruit butter is an old style pride. They use a exquisite deal less sugar than jams and jellies, and the fruit is cooked with out adding pectin. Instead, the obviously taking place pectin observed in fruits allows the butter to thicken and jell. As a quit end end result, fruit butter is generally greater spreadable than jams or jellies. Another plus is that fruit butter can be made using a whole lot less than ideal fruit which consist of providence apples and pears that haven't commenced to rot. You will, but, want to reduce out any bruised spots or rotten regions.

The approach for making fruit butter is first to prepare dinner dinner the fruit to make pulp. Then you'll add sugar and spices to the pulp and hold to put together dinner till it's ready to can. Fruit butter is simple to prepare, but it does take time to finish the cooking approach.

Preparing the Fruit Pulp Apple might be the maximum common fruit butter, however you may additionally make fantastic butter from apricots, grapes, peaches, pears, and plums. When making fruit butter, you will need to apply ripe fruit that has been washed thoroughly and had any bruising removed.

Apples: Quarter apples. No want to center or peel them. (Much of an apple's herbal pectin is determined inside the center.) Add half as hundreds apple juice or cider as you've got were given were given fruit.

Apricots: Remove pits after which overwhelm the fruit. Add half of as a brilliant deal water or juice as you have fruit.

Grapes: Remove stems after which overwhelm the fruit. No want to function more liquid.

Peaches: Peel by using way of immersing peaches in boiling water for about 30– 60 seconds or until the pores and pores and skin loosens quick. Remove pits after which crush the fruit. No need to feature greater liquid.

Pears: Remove stem and blossom ends. Peel if favored. Quarter and middle the pears and then weigh down the fruit. No want to add extra liquid.

Plums: Remove pits after which crush the fruit. No want to feature more liquid.

Cook your prepared fruit, often stirring, so it doesn't scorch or keep on with the pan. The fruit wishes to be cooked till it's far very soft and looks thick. This can take an hour or extra. Next, run the cooked fruit via a sieve or meals mill to puree the pulp and take away the peelings, seeds, and so forth.

Basic Fruit Butter Recipe Measure out your fruit pulp and add ½ cup sugar, greater or an entire lot a great deal less to taste, in line with cup of pulp.

Add ½ to at least one tsp. Ground cinnamon in line with quart of pulp and ⅛ tsp. Per quart of each different spices, you preference to use, together with allspice, cloves, nutmeg, and ginger.

Place the puree in a massive, heavy kettle (a thin-walled pot will have a tendency to scorch the butter because it cooks). The kettle ought to have immoderate sufficient elements that the butter obtained't boil over even as cooking down, and the wider the lowest of the kettle, the extra evaporation is probably capable of take location, therefore producing a thick butter in an awful lot less time.

Cook the butter over medium-low warm temperature, continuously stirring, till sugar is dissolved and the fruit starts offevolved to boil. Continue cooking, stirring very frequently, till the butter thickens. The butter is prepared while it rounds barely on a spoon and has a smooth sheen.

When the butter is prepared, you're now prepared to can it. Pack the new butter into sterilized warm pint jars, leaving ¼ inch headspace. Place the lids and bands on and machine in a boiling water-bathtub canner for 10 minutes.

Apple butter is probably the most customarily-made fruit butter, and cinnamon is the standard spice brought. Try together with nutmeg or ginger for a tasty variant whilst making pear butter. And even as you're making grape, peach, or apricot, there's no want to add any more spices—they will be actual. Cook's preference!

Fruit/Applesauce Butter

This is an thrilling and attractive recipe I were given years in the beyond from a Plain lady at the church I attended. It gives a piece of a flavor version from the greater traditional butter.

eight cups applesauce

One large package deal of Jell-O (i.E., strawberry or raspberry)

One small bundle of unflavored gelatin (non-obligatory)

If the usage of, dissolve Jell-O in ½ cup boiling water and dissolve unflavored gelatin in ½ cup bloodless water. Mix after which upload the applesauce; heat to a simmer after which positioned the fruit/applesauce butter into pint jars and gadget them in a boiling water bath for 10 mins, following the Step-by using-Step Guide.

Jams

Fruit jams make an awesome addition in your menus, and in Amish kitchens, you'll regularly find bread and jam or jelly at most food because they assist to "fill in the corners" of great appetites. Holes moreover make terrific toppings for pancakes, biscuits, angel meals cake, or perhaps ice cream.

Whereas jelly is made from fruit juice, jam is made the usage of beaten fruit. The hollow is generally softer than jelly, and at the identical time as it will more or much less preserve its form at the same time as spooned onto a chunk of bread, it may be effortlessly unfold, even on a sensitive object. Plus, you obtained't want as a outstanding deal fruit to make a batch of jam due to the truth you'll be using the fruit meat rather than genuinely the juice. Also, you can use frozen fruit that has been thawed, so your options are even greater enormous.

Making Jam Without Added Pectin

There are severa techniques to test for doneness at the same time as cooking jam, but to my way of wondering, the most dependable technique is that this:

•Using a sweet thermometer, first boil a pot of plain water. Insert the thermometer into the boiling water to determine the actual temperature. Water boils at slightly particular temperatures relying to your elevation and the present day-day atmospheric situations. So, to be as accurate as feasible, it's an splendid concept to take the boiling water temperature whenever you suggest to make a jam.

•In a big pot, mix the overwhelmed fruit and sugar in line with the recipes under and then deliver the combination to a boil, stirring very often. Keep the warm temperature exceedingly low till the sugar has simply dissolved, and then flip the heat as much as prepare dinner the jam . When the hole temperature has risen 9 levels higher than the temperature at which the obvious water boiled, it has reached its jelling aspect and is now geared up to be processed. Immediately take the pot off the warmth.

•Let the jam take a seat down for 4 to 5 minutes, gently stirring regularly so you received't create air bubbles in a jam. This will help the bits of fruit to stoop in the path of the jam in region of gathering at the pinnacle.

•Ladle jam into warmth sterilized pint or half of-pint jars, leaving ¼-inch headspace. Put the lids and bands on and system in a boiling water bath for 15 minutes. (Refer to the Step-through-Step Guide for water-bathtub canning.)

Jam Recipes Using No Added Pectin

The following recipes are for making jam with out including packaged pectin. When choosing your fruit, try and have approximately 1 / 4 of the amount wished a chunk under-ripe. Slightly below-ripe fruit has extra natural pectin than sincerely ripened fruit, and your jams may be thicker.

If you don't thoughts some surprises along the way, you could strive your hand at any fruit (or combos of fruit) to be had. Make notes about what labored and what did now not, and boom your personal recipes.

Apricot Jam

2 quarts peeled, pitted, and beaten apricots

¼ cup lemon juice

6 cups sugar

In a massive pot, integrate beaten apricots and lemon juice and stir to combine. Add sugar and stir to combine and dissolve. Follow the instructions for "Making Jam with out Added Pectin."

Berry Jam (blackberry, blueberry, boysenberry, raspberry, and so forth.)

nine cups overwhelmed berries

6 cups sugar

Follow the directions for "Making Jam with out Added Pectin."

Concord Grape Jam

(Note: Concord grapes have seeds, but they may be a "slip pores and skin" variety, this means that that that you may pop the grapes out of their skins via gently squeezing them. Kids want to assist! Concord grapes make excellent juice, jelly, jam, and butter due to the deep pink color of the skins and remarkable flavor.)

2 quarts of stemmed Concord grapes

6 cups sugar

Pop the grapes from the skins and set them apart. Chop the skins in a food processor, chopper, or blender and add ½ cup water; cook dinner the combination of skins and water gently on low warmth for approximately 20 minutes.

Meanwhile, put together dinner the now-skinless grapes in each unique pot until they may be smooth and may be pushed via a sieve or great-mesh strainer to cast off the seeds. Work in batches whilst straining to get as lots pulp as feasible.

Combine the grape pulp, skins, and sugar and produce to a boil, following the instructions in "Making Jam with out Added Pectin."

Peach Jam

2 quarts peeled and crushed peaches

½ cup water

6 cups sugar

In a big pot, combine the peaches and water and prepare dinner lightly for 10 mins. (The softened fruit is less complex to weigh down.) Add sugar and follow the guidelines in "Making Jam without Added Pectin."

Pineapple Jam

2 quarts finely chopped pineapple (peeled and cored)

5 cups sugar

One lemon, thinly sliced and seeded

2 cups water

In a huge pot, placed all the additives together and bring to a boil, following commands in "Making Jam with out Added Pectin."

Strawberry Jam

2 quarts of beaten strawberries

6 cups sugar

In a big pot, combine strawberries and sugar and then deliver to a boil, following the pointers in "Making Jam without Added Pectin."

Making Jam with Added Pectin

First of all, a be aware approximately packaged pectin: Powdered pectin and liquid pectin are present. Powdered pectin has an prolonged shelf lifestyles, so if you buy a amount of pectin on sale, powdered will final longer on your pantry. Just make certain to test the "use with the aid of" date because of the fact pectin does lose its jelling potential over the years. Also, powdered pectin is generally combined with the unheated beaten fruit, and liquid pectin is added to the cooked fruit and sugar aggregate proper now after it is taken off the warm temperature. Cooking time is the same for both merchandise—four minutes at a whole rolling boil even as stirring constantly.

Your results may be greater consistent even as you use pectin for your jam recipes, notwithstanding the fact that there is constantly the risk that you could have a set failure. Call it syrup, and apply it to pancakes or ice cream whilst that happens. It will nevertheless taste proper!

Step-with the aid of-Step Directions for Making Jam

•Fill your water-tub canner midway with water and set the warmth low to supply the water to a simmer.

•Wash and sterilize your jars and keep them heat till you want them, each for your heated dishwasher or by the use of using fame them up for your clean sink or a large pot and pouring boiling water over them to cover. When prepared to apply, drain the jars earlier than filling them with the jam.

•Put the screw bands and lids in a pot and cowl them with water. Bring water to a simmer—don't boil!—and depart them till equipped to use.

•Prepare the fruit. A potato masher works thoroughly for crushing most end quit end result. The reason is to have tiny bits of overwhelmed fruit further to the juice that's released eventually of crushing without pureeing. •Using a liquid measuring field, diploma the quantity of organized fruit and placed it in a huge pot (at the least 6 to 8 quarts). Stir in lemon juice or water if the recipe calls for it.

•If powdered pectin is used, stir it into the overwhelmed fruit now. If using liquid pectin, you will add it after the cooking is entire.

•Measure out the sugar you may be the use of and set it apart for now.

•Bring aggregate to a whole rolling boil on high warm temperature while stirring constantly.

•Quickly stir within the sugar and go returned to a complete rolling boil. Boil for four minutes, stirring continuously.

•Remove from warmth. If the use of liquid pectin, stir it in now.

•Allow the jam to simply accept 4 to five minutes, from time to time stirring so the fruit doesn't go with the flow on top of the liquid. Skim off any foam the usage of a steel spoon, making your jam prettier in the jar.

•Quickly ladle the jam into your easy, warmness jars, filling to interior ⅛ inch of the top.

•Wipe the jar rims and threads using a moist paper towel or material and cowl with the two-piece lids, screwing the bands on tight.

•Place the jars in the canner, making sure a rack on the bottom to raise the jars off the pot's ground. Water ought to cowl the tops of the jars thru 1 to 2 inches; if important, upload boiling water.

• Boil the water in a included canner.

• Process bottlenecks embody the following:

Altitude in Feet	Processing Time
0 – 1,000	10 minutes
1,001 – 3,000	15 minutes
3,001 – 6,000	20 minutes
6,001 – 8,000	25 minutes
8,001 – 10,000	30 minutes

• When processing is over, take the jars out of the canner and vicinity them on a folded towel or a board to take a seat returned in reality. Check whether a seal have become installed as quickly because the jars have truly cooled: the middle of the lid want to be down, and at the same time as you push the top together together with your finger, there need to be no movement in the cover, and it want to no longer get higher up at the equal time as pressed. If a jar does no longer seal efficaciously, it should be refrigerated and consumed internal 3 weeks.

• Allow the jam jars to rest at room temperature for twenty-four hours in advance than casting off the screw bands. Check to ensure that a enough seal have become shaped, then wipe down before storing the lids and jars. Some jams will take around weeks to set successfully, but you may use them right away if you want.

Recipes for Jam with Added Pectin

Powdered Pectin Apricot Jam

5 cups pitted apricots, sort of chopped or beaten; skins left on ½ cup lemon juice

1 pound powdered pectin

eight cups sugar

For processing instructions, see "Step-via-Step Directions for Making Jam with Added Pectin." This recipe yields round 5 quarts (pints).

Blackberry Jam with Liquid Pectin

four cups crushed blackberries

4 cup lemon juice

7 cups sugar

One pouch pectin liquid

If desired, overwhelm the berries and sift about half of of of of the pulp to remove a number of the seeds. According to the "Step-thru-Step Directions for Making Jam with Added Pectin", do not forget no longer to function the liquid pectin till the cooking is finished. This recipe yields spherical four quarts (pints).

Blackberry Jam with Powdered Pectin

6 cups crushed blackberries

1 pound powdered pectin

14 cups of clean lemon juice

8½ cup sugar

If desired, weigh down the berries and sift about 1/2 of the pulp to take away some of the seeds. According to the "Step-by using the use of manner of-Step Directions for Making Jam with Added Pectin." This recipe yields approximately 6 quarts.

Blueberry Jam with Powdered Pectin

3¾ cup beaten blueberries

One packet of powdered pectin

¼ cup lemon juice

1 cup of water

6 cups sugar

According to the "Step-through-Step Directions for Making Jam with Added Pectin." This recipe yields round 4 quarts.

Blueberry/Raspberry Jam with Powdered Pectin

three cups blueberries

3 cups raspberries

¼ cup lemon juice

One challenge of pectin powder

7 cups sugar

According to the "Step-with the useful resource of-Step Directions for Making Jam with Added Pectin." This recipe yields about 6 quarts.

(Ground or Sour) Cherry Jam with Liquid Pectin

4½ cup finely minced crushed cherries or pitted sour cherries, stems eliminated, ¼ cup clean lemon juice

7 cups sugar

Two liquid pectin pouches

According to the "Step-with the resource of-Step Directions for Making Jam with Added Pectin",; endure in mind now not to characteristic the liquid pectin till the cooking is completed. This recipe yields round 4 quarts.

(Sour or Ground) Cherry Jam with Powdered Pectin

four cups ground cherries or pitted sour cherries, coarsely minced stems removed, ¼ cup clean lemon juice

1 pound powdered pectin

5 cups sugar

According to the "Step-via manner of-Step Directions for Making Jam with Added Pectin." This recipe yields round 3 quarts.

(Sweet) Cherry Jam with Powdered Pectin

3 cups candy cherries, coarsely chopped

½ cup sparkling lemon juice

4½ cup sugar

According to the "Step-via-Step Directions for Making Jam with Added Pectin." This recipe yields spherical 2½ quarts.

Liquid Pectin with Fig Jam

4 cups smashed figs, and stem ends eliminated

½ cup glowing lemon juice

7½ cup sugar

One pouch pectin liquid

According to the "Step-with the useful resource of-Step Directions for Making Jam With Added Pectin",; don't forget now not to function the liquid pectin until the cooking is completed. This recipe yields spherical 4 quarts.

Powdered Pectin with Nectarine Jam

five cups peeled, pitted, and coarsely chopped or beaten nectarines ½ cup glowing lemon juice

1 pound powdered pectin

7 cups sugar

According to the "Step-with the useful resource of-Step Directions for Making Jam With Added Pectin." This recipe yields round 4½ quarts.

Liquid Pectin Peach Jam

4½ cup peeled, pitted, and smashed peaches

¼ cup lemon juice

7 cups sugar

1 to two oz... Candied ginger, coarsely chopped (non-compulsory)

One pouch pectin liquid

According to the "Step-with the aid of-Step Directions for Making Jam With Added Pectin", consider now not to add the liquid pectin until the cooking is finished. This recipe yields round four quarts.

Powdered Pectin with Peach Jam

3¾ cup peeled, pitted, and smashed peaches

¼ cup lemon juice

1 pound powdered pectin

5 cups sugar

According to the "Step-thru using-Step Directions for Making Jam With Added Pectin." Make about three quarts.

Liquid Pectin with Pear Jam

4 cups pears, peeled, cored, and coarsely chopped

¼ cup glowing lemon juice

7 cups sugar

Two liquid pectin pouches

According to the "Step-with the useful resource of manner of-Step Directions for Making Jam With Added Pectin"; go through in thoughts now not to characteristic the liquid pectin till the cooking is finished. This recipe yields spherical four quarts.

Powdered Pectin with Pear Jam

four cups peeled, cored, and coarsely chopped pears

¼ cup lemon juice

One packet of powdered pectin

8½ cups sugar

According to the "Step-with the aid of-Step Directions for Making Jam With Added Pectin." This recipe yields spherical 3½ quarts.

Liquid Pectin with Pineapple Jam

One crushed pineapple can (20 ounces..)

Three tablespoons of lemon juice

3¼ cup sugar

One pouch pectin liquid

According to the "Step-through the use of-Step Directions for Making Jam With Added Pectin", keep in thoughts no longer to function the liquid pectin until the cooking is completed. This recipe yields around 2 quarts.

Liquid Pectin with Plum Jam

4½ cup plums pitted and smashed or coarsely chopped

¼ cup glowing lemon juice

7½ cups sugar

One pouch pectin liquid

According to the "Step-thru-Step Directions for Making Jam With Added Pectin", don't forget no longer to feature the liquid pectin until the cooking is finished. This recipe yields round 4 quarts.

Powdered Pectin with Plum Jam

6 cups pitted and overwhelmed or coarsely diced plums

¼ cup lemon juice

1 pound powdered pectin

eight cups sugar

According to the "Step-by manner of way of-Step Directions for Making Jam with Added Pectin." This recipe yields spherical 4½ quarts.

Rhubarb Jam with Powdered Pectin

6 cups prepared rhubarb (see instructions beneath)

One packet of powdered pectin

8½ cups sugar

Rhubarb training: Cut four pounds of red-stalk rhubarb into half of-inch quantities. Add 2¼ cup water and ¼ cup lemon juice to a boil. Cook and cowl until very mild, stirring every so often. Proceed with the recipe after measuring out 6 cups.

According to the "Step-thru-Step Directions for Making Jam With Added Pectin." This recipe yields around five quarts.

Rhubarb/Strawberry Jam with Liquid Pectin

1 cup rhubarb, organized (see tips under)

2½ dozen overwhelmed strawberries

6½ cups sugar

One pouch pectin liquid

Rhubarb schooling: 1 pound red-stalk rhubarb reduce into 1/2-inch quantities. Bring ¼ cup water and 3 teaspoons of lemon juice to a boil. Cook and cover until very moderate, stirring every now and then. Proceed with the recipe after measuring out 1 cup.

According to the "Step-with the resource of manner of-Step Directions for Making Jam With Added Pectin", endure in thoughts not to function the liquid pectin until the cooking is completed. M makes about 3½ pints.

Liquid Pectin with Strawberry Jam

four cups mashed strawberries

¼ cup clean lemon juice

7 cups sugar

One pouch pectin liquid

According to the "Step-through the use of-Step Directions for Making Jam With Added Pectin", do not forget now not to function the liquid pectin until the cooking is finished. This recipe yields spherical four quarts.

Powdered Pectin Strawberry Jam

5½ cup shredded strawberries

¼ cup lemon juice

1 pound powdered pectin

8 cups sugar

According to the "Step-with the aid of-Step Directions for Making Jam With Added Pectin." This recipe yields round five quarts.

Jellies

Even in the event that they in no way can something else, many human beings make a batch or of jelly each 12 months. Jelly is an awesome way to get commenced out with canning and could not take prolonged if you buy your juice in desire to extracting it from the fruit. Make certain that any juice you purchase to deliver jelly is a hundred percent juice and no longer using a delivered sugar or corn syrup. I almost usually buy grape juice for jelly-making, and I've in recent times made jelly the use of sold bottles of pomegranate, black cherry, and raspberry juice. Various mixed juices are to be had in recent times and is probably have emerge as jelly. Why no longer strive a blueberry/raspberry or a cranberry/apple mixture? The flavor combos you may create are nearly countless. Another advantage of buying juice is that you can make jelly any time of 12 months—no want to wait until the fruit is ripe inside the summer time.

Fruit Preparation and Juice Extraction

Make the fruit: Wash the fruit with the useful resource of both going for walks bloodless water over it or filling a basin or big difficulty with bloodless water severa times and submerging after which pulling the fruit out on every occasion. You do not want to head away the fruit within the water for too lengthy.

The approach for extracting juice varies based totally on the form of fruit being processed. Juicy berries may be beaten and the juice extracted without heating, however stiff fruit want to be cooked to soften it and start the glide of liquid, and a few water want to be frequently introduced while the fruit is boiled.

Take out the juice: After you have got prepped the fruit, it is time to split the juice from the pulp. Place the prepared fruit in a fruit press or clean out, a jelly bag (hose down the bag before including the fruit pulp), or a double layer of moistened cheesecloth. Allow the fruit to drop even as amassing the juice.

Allowing the fruit to empty without squeezing or twisting the bag outcomes in smooth juice, which paperwork the maximum endearing jelly. However, it offers the least quantity of liquid, so you can also desire to expose the bag of fruit tightly or compress and press the bag to extract as tons juice as feasible. If you use a fruit press or strainer, you have to clean out the juice yet again, the usage of a double thickness of moistened cheesecloth and allowing the liquid to trickle through without squeezing or twisting. This will genuinely smooth the liquid.

Making Pectin with delivered Jelly

Pectin is available in office work: powdered and liquid, as we observed in the very last lesson on getting geared up jam. Powdered pectin is mixed with unheated fruit juice, at the identical time as liquid pectin is used with the boiling juice and sugar mixture. The boiling time for any shape of pectin is the same—2 minutes at a complete rolling boil (a boil that cannot be delivered down).

Pectin is important in conducting a proper set for the purpose that jelly need to be difficult sufficient to maintain its shape while sliced. It is feasible to prepare jelly without greater pectin, as pioneer ladies did, however it seems a pity no longer to use the notably to be had packaged pectin. So, in every of the following recipes, you can use powdered or liquid pectin.

Step-thru-Step Instructions for Making Jelly

• Fill your water-tub canner midway with water and positioned it to a simmer over low heat.

• Wash and sterilize your jars, then keep them warmth for your heated dishwasher or with the aid of popularity them up in a easy sink or massive pot and pouring boiling water over them to cowl. When organized to use, drain the jars thoroughly in advance than filling them with the jelly.

• Cover the screw bands and lids with water in a saucepan. Bring the water to a simmer (do now not boil!) and preserve it there until ready to apply.

• Prepare the fruit and squeeze out the juice.

• Measure out the right amount of prepared fruit juice the use of a liquid measuring jug and location it in a huge saucepan (as a minimum 6 to eight quarts). If the recipe asks for it, add lemon juice or water.

• If the usage of powdered pectin, upload it proper away to the juice. If using liquid pectin, upload it after the cooking is completed.

• Measure out the sugar you could use in a unique bowl and leave it aside for now.

- Cook over excessive warm temperature, stirring regularly, till the mixture reaches a complete rolling boil.

- Return to a entire rolling boil after rapid stirring in the sugar. 2 minutes of boiling, constant stirring

- Remove from the warmth. If you're using liquid pectin, add it now.

- Quickly skim off the froth earlier than ladling the jelly into easy, warm jars, filling to inner 18 inches of the top.

- Before masking with the two-piece lids and tightening the bands, clean the jar rims and threads with wet paper towels or cloths.

Altitude in Feet	Processing Time
0 – 1,000	5 minutes
1,001 – 3,000	10 minutes
3,001 – 6,000	15 minutes
6,001 – 8,000	20 minutes
8,001 – 10,000	25 minutes

- Place the jars inside the canner, ensuring a rack on the lowest to elevate the jars off the pot's ground. Water ought to cover the tops of the jars thru the usage of 1 to 2 inches; if essential, upload boiling water to cowl the jar tops nicely.

- Boil the water in a included canner.

- Make the jelly as follows:

- When processing is over, take the jars out of the canner and area them on a folded towel or a board to sit back completely. Check to peer whether or not or now not a seal advanced as soon as the jars have completely cooled: the center of the lid want to be down, and while you push the duvet along with your finger, there want to be no motion in the cowl, and it must now not get better up while pressed. If a jar does now not seal successfully, it ought to be refrigerated and ate up inner 3 weeks.

- Allow the jelly jars to stand at room temperature for twenty-four hours in advance than removing the screw bands, double-checking for a right seal, and wiping off the lids and jars before garage.

Recipes for Individual Jellies

Remember! You can also moreover constantly purchase the juice for the recipes under. Simply bypass the stairs for extracting the juice from the fruit and go to the jelly-making step. It's honest!

Liquid Pectin with Blackberry Jelly

4 cups glowing blackberry juice (from approximately 3 quarts of berries, stems, and caps eliminated)

2 tsp lemon juice

7½ cup sugar

Two liquid pectin pouches

Crush the berries and extract the juice as directed in "Preparing Fruit and Extracting the Juice," or boil the berries first if desired.

According to the "Step-via using manner of-Step Directions for Making Jelly," do not upload the liquid pectin till the cooking is finished. This recipe yields round 4 quarts.

Powdered Pectin Blackberry Jelly

3½ cup blackberry juice (about 2–2½ quarts of berries, stems, and tops removed)

5 cups sugar

1 pound powdered pectin

2 T. Lemon juice

Crush the berries and extract the juice as directed in "Preparing Fruit and Extracting the Juice," or boil the berries first if desired.

The technique consistent with the "Step-by using the usage of-Step Directions for Making Jelly." This recipe yields spherical 3 quarts.

Powdered Pectin with Boysenberry Jelly

3½ cup blueberry juice (from about three quarts of berries)

1 pound powdered pectin

2 T. Lemon juice

five cups sugar

Crush the berries and extract the juice as directed in "Preparing Fruit and Extracting the Juice," or boil the berries first if desired.

According to the "Step-with the resource of-Step Directions for Making Jelly." This recipe yields round 2½ quarts.

Liquid Pectin with Cherry Jelly

3 cups cherry juice (crafted from 2 quarts sour or pie cherries and ½ cup water)

7 cups sugar

Two liquid pectin pouches

If you stem cherries, you do no longer want to pit them. Place cherries in a huge saucepan and crush them. Bring the water to a boil over excessive warmth, included. Reduce the warm temperature to low and simmer for about 10 mins earlier than extracting the juice, as defined in "Preparing Fruit and Extracting Juice."

According to the "Step-with the aid of-Step Directions for Making Jelly," do not add the liquid pectin till the cooking is finished. This recipe yields spherical 4 quarts.

Powdered Pectin with Cherry Jelly

3½ cup cherry juice (crafted from approximately 2 quarts of bitter or pie cherries and ½ cup water)

1 pound powdered pectin

4½ cup sugar

If you stem cherries, you do now not need to pit them. Place cherries in a large saucepan and crush them. Bring the water to a boil over excessive warmth, blanketed. Reduce the warmth to low and simmer for approximately 10 mins earlier than extracting the juice, as described in "Preparing Fruit and Extracting Juice."

According to the "Step-via-Step Directions for Making Jelly." This recipe yields spherical three quarts.

Liquid Pectin Currant Jelly

5 cup purple currant juice (from round 5 pounds of fruit)

7 cups sugar

One pouch pectin liquid

Crush the currants and, if wanted, warm temperature to assist in extracting the juice, as defined in "Preparing Fruit and Extracting the Juice."

According to the "Step-via-Step Directions for Making Jelly," do no longer add the liquid pectin till the cooking is finished. This recipe yields round four quarts.

Liquid Pectin with Elderberry Jelly

four cup elderberry juice (from about 3 pints berries, stalks eliminated)

7½ cup sugar

2 T. Lime juice

Two liquid pectin pouches

Heat the berries earlier than crushing them, taking care not to burn them. Crush berries and juice as directed in "Preparing Fruit and Extracting Juice."

According to the "Step-through-Step Directions for Making Jelly," do not add the liquid pectin till the cooking is completed. This recipe yields spherical four quarts.

Powdered Pectin with Elderberry Jelly

6 cups sugar

3½ cup elderberry juice (from around 2½ quarts berries, stems eliminated)

1 pound powdered pectin

2 T. Lemon juice

Heat the berries earlier than crushing them, taking care no longer to burn them. Crush berries and juice as directed in "Preparing Fruit and Extracting Juice."

According to the "Step-by way of way of-Step Directions for Making Jelly." This recipe yields round three quarts.

Liquid Pectin Grape Jelly

four cup grape juice (made from 3½ pounds of Concord grapes and ½ cup water)

7 cups sugar

One pouch pectin liquid

Grapes must be stemmed after which overwhelmed. Add the grapes and water to a massive saucepan, cowl, and bring to a boil over excessive warmth. Using low warm temperature, simmer for spherical 10 minutes. Extract the juice as directed in "Preparing Fruit and Extracting the Juice."

According to the "Step-thru-Step Directions for Making Jelly," do not add the liquid pectin till the cooking is finished. This recipe yields spherical 4½ quarts.

Powdered Pectin with Grape Jelly

One packet of powdered pectin

five cups grape juice (from round 3½ pounds Concord grapes and 1 cup water)

7 cups sugar

Grapes need to be stemmed after which overwhelmed. Add the grapes and water to a large saucepan, cowl, and bring to a boil over excessive warmness. Simmer for round 10 mins on low warm temperature. Extract the juice as directed in "Preparing Fruit and Extracting the Juice."

According to the "Step-by using way of-Step Directions for Making Jelly." This recipe yields spherical five quarts.

Liquid Pectin with Mint Jelly

1 cup chopped mint leaves and touchy stems, well packed to degree

1 cup of water

½ cup apple cider vinegar and 3½ cup sugar

Five drops of food coloring, green

One pouch pectin liquid

Mint leaves ought to be washed and prepared. Fill a huge pot halfway with mint. Stir within the vinegar, water, and sugar. Stir regularly because of the truth the combination involves a complete rolling boil over immoderate warm temperature. Return to a excessive rolling boil and boil for 30 seconds after collectively with the meals coloring and pectin.

Remove from the warm temperature and, running unexpectedly, skim and stress the jelly through layers of wet cheesecloth. Fill jars halfway with strained jelly and method according to the "Step-with the useful aid of-Step Directions for Making Jelly." This recipe yields round 2 quarts.

Powdered Pectin with Pepper Jelly

three cups freshly squeezed pepper juice (from about one lb. Warm peppers, or a aggregate of warmth and bell peppers, which encompass the vinegar and water used to put together the juice; see under)

1 pound powdered pectin

4 cups sugar

3 to 5 drops of green or purple meals coloring, counting on juice shade (non-obligatory)

Remove the stems and seeds from the peppers. 2 cups finely chopped or floor peppers (you could pulse in a food processor or Vitamix) in a huge saucepan, 2 cups of water, and 1 cup of apple cider vinegar.

For about 15 mins, supply to a boil, lower warmth, cover, and simmer. You may additionally moreover either use the juice with the pepper debris or clean out it through many layers of moist cheesecloth. According to the "Step-thru-Step Directions for Making Jelly." This recipe yields round 2½ quarts.

Liquid Pectin with Plum Jelly

four cup plum juice (made from 4½ kilos of plums and ½ cup water)

7½ cup sugar

One pouch pectin liquid

No want to peel or pit plums; reduce them into quantities. Crush the plum portions in a mixing bowl, upload the water, cowl, and convey to a boil over excessive warm temperature. Reduce the warmth to low and simmer for 10 mins to extract the juice, as directed in "Preparing Fruit and Extracting the Juice."

According to the "Step-via-Step Directions for Making Jelly," do now not add the liquid pectin until the cooking is completed. This recipe yields round four quarts.

Powdered Pectin with Plum Jelly

One packet of powdered pectin

5 cups plum juice (from 4½ kilos plums and 1 cup water)

7 cups sugar

No want to peel or pit plums; really lessen them into quantities. Crush the plum portions in a mixing bowl, upload the water, cowl, and produce to a boil over excessive warmth. Reduce the warm temperature to low and simmer for 10 minutes to extract the juice, as directed in "Preparing Fruit and Extracting the Juice."

According to the "Step-with the aid of-Step Directions for Making Jelly." Makes 3½ to 4 pints.

Powdered Pectin Pomegranate Jelly

One area of powdered pectin

3½ cup pomegranate juice (from around ten pomegranates)

five cups sugar

If you invest in shop-sold juice, this is the recipe for that you have to acquire this. However, if you need to extract the juice from glowing pomegranates, split them in 1/2 of of and then use a juice reamer (much like the most effective used to juice a lemon or orange) to interrupt the berries and launch the juice. Proceed after straining the liquid via numerous layers of moist cheesecloth.

According to the "Step-by means of using the use of-Step Directions for Making Jelly." This recipe yields round three quarts.

Powdered Pectin Raspberry Jelly

One concern of powdered pectin

4 cups raspberry juice (from round three quarts of fruit)

5 cups sugar

Crush the berries and extract the juice as directed in "Preparing Fruit and Extracting the Juice," or boil the berries first if desired.

According to the "Step-through-Step Directions for Making Jelly." This recipe yields round 3 quarts.

Liquid Pectin with Strawberry Jelly

4 cups easy strawberry juice (from approximately three quarts of berries, stems, and caps eliminated)

7½ cup sugar

2 tsp lemon juice

Two liquid pectin pouches

Crush the berries and extract the juice as directed in "Preparing Fruit and Extracting the Juice," or boil the berries first if favored.

According to the "Step-with the aid of-Step Directions for Making Jelly," do not upload the liquid pectin till the cooking is completed. This recipe yields spherical 4 quarts.

Powdered Pectin with Strawberry Jelly

3½ cup strawberry juice (crafted from approximately 2½ quarts of berries, stalks, and tops eliminated)

4½ cup sugar

1 pound powdered pectin

2 T. Lime juice

Crush the berries and extract the juice as directed in "Preparing Fruit and Extracting the Juice," or boil the berries first if favored.

According to the "Step-with the aid of manner of-Step Directions for Making Jelly." This recipe yields spherical 3 quarts.

Amish White Bread

What substances you can need:

1/four ounce dry yeast

half of cup water

2 teaspoons salt

1/3 cup sugar

2 cups water

2 1/2 of of tablespoons shortening

1/eight-1/four cup butter

6 -7 cups bread flour or all motive flour

Directions:

1) Take ½ cup of heat water and droop yeast in it.

2) In a huge-sized bowl, aggregate in salt, sugar, 2 cups of water and shortening. Add within the yeast combination and mix properly.

3) Slowly add in flour just so to form dough. Flour a surface and turn down the dough on it. Knead it perfectly till it smoothens.

four) Grease a bowl and permit the dough upward push in it for two hours. Don't neglect about to cowl it. Once it rises, punch it down and divide into same loaves.

5) Take a 9x5 inched loaf pan and grease it. Put the divided dough in it and with the help of a fork, prick the pinnacle lightly.

6) Allow it to upward push for minimal 2 hours or till the dough is better than the pan. Bake it for half-hour at 375 stages.

7) Once it's completed, permit it to chill for 10 minutes and then butter the pinnacle of the loaves with a brush.

8) Let the pans relaxation till the loaves depart the sides of it. Remove the loaves from the pans and allow them to rest for some time.

9) Serve and enjoy .This recipe will provide you with 24 servings in fashionable.

Nutritional records in line with serving:

Calories: 145kcal

Carbohydrates: 25g

Protein: 4g

Fat: 3g

Fiber: 1g

= = = = = = = = = = = = = = = = = = = =

Delicious Soft Pretzels, Amish Recipe

What materials you could want:

1 1/4 cups water

1 tablespoon yeast

2 cups flour

2 cups occident flour (bread flour)

1/four cup brown sugar

Dipping answer

three cups warmth water

half of cup baking soda

Sweet creamy butter

Directions:

1) Take heat water and mix in yeast with it; until nicely dissolved. Then add in sugar and flour and stir flawlessly.

2) You don't must "knead" it because it will bring about thickening the dough!

three) Leave it for 20 mins in order that it may upward push and then reduce into rope shapes. Cut them into pretzels form and then dunk them into the dipping sauce.

4) Grease a cookie sheet gently and installation the pretzels on it. Dust with some pretzel salt.

five) Bake in oven for four-6 minutes at 500-550 degrees F. Take them out once they gather a moderate brown color. Dip the pinnacle of pretzel into the melted butter.

6) Variation: You can upload 1tsp of vanilla to the dough in case you want.

7) Flavor Variations:

8) Cinnamon/sugar: Skip salt and dip the pretzels into cinnamon sugar after the face has been included with the melted butter.

nine) Sour Cream & Onion: After dipping it in melted butter, dirt a few sour cream and onion on it.

10) Powder Garlic: The technique may be as for the bitter cream and onion, simply use garlic powder!

eleven) Sesame or Poppy Seed: This have to be completed in advance than baking-after you've got dipped the pretzels inside the dipping solution, dip the face of the pretzels into seeds and then hold for baking. Salt isn't always compulsory with this one.

10) Serve and enjoy .This recipe will give you 24 servings in wellknown.

Nutritional facts consistent with serving:

Calories: 86kcal

Carbohydrates: 18g

Protein: 3g

Fat: 0g

Fiber: 1g

= = = = = = = = = = = = = = = = = = = =

Amish Baked Oatmeal

What components you could need:

1 half of cups quick cooking oatmeal

half of of cup milk

1/2 cup sugar

1/4 cup melted butter

1 teaspoon baking powder

3/4 teaspoon salt

1 egg

1 teaspoon vanilla extract

Directions:

1) First of all preheat oven to 350 degrees F. In this recipe use a 13 x 9 length pan and make it little greasy earlier than baking approach.

2) Put all components in a mixing bowl and mix them well.

3) Pour this combination inside the greasy pan and then located it in to preheated oven for baking system. Now bake it in oven for 1/2-hour till it turns into golden brown.

four) After baking add it within the bowl and then pour heat milk in it. You can add some sparkling stop result in it too.

5) This recipe will offer 6 servings in fashionable.

Nutritional information in step with serving:

Calories: 230kcal

Carbohydrates: 30g

Protein: 5g

Fat: 10g

Fiber: 2g

= = = = = = = = = = = = = = = = = = = =

Amish Bread for the Bread Machine

What elements you may need:

1 1/8 cup water

half of teaspoon salt

1/4 cup sugar

1/4 cup oil

1 teaspoon yeast

2 three/4 cups bread flour

Directions:

1) First of all add water and salt within the bread device. Then add sugar and flour in it and ultimately upload yeast in gadget.

2) On first step select easy bread cycle and transfer off it at the same time because it completes 2nd rising.

3) Restart it Again and choose essential cycle this time too.

4) Cook it with normal way.

Nutritional statistics steady with serving:

Calories: 400kcal

Carbohydrates: 70g

Protein: 10g

Fat: 10g

Fiber: 3g

= = = = = = = = = = = = = = = = = = = =

Amish Oven-Fried Chicken

What additives you will need:

1/three cup vegetable oil

1 teaspoon dried marjoram

10 bird quantities

1 teaspoon garlic salt

2 teaspoons paprika

2 teaspoons black pepper

1 teaspoon salt

1 cup all purpose flour

1/three cup butter

Directions:

1) Take a shallow cooking pan and upload oil and butter in it. Place the cooking pan in an oven at 375 levels F, on the way to melt the butter. Once it's achieved, placed it sideways.

2) Take a large paper sack and integrate all the dry components in it.

three) For the bird pieces; roll them (three quantities at a time) in butter and oil and region them in a sack and shake well.

4) Arrange them on a plate at the same time as finished. Leave the excessive oil and butter aggregate within the pan.

5) Put the chicken piece inside the pan (with pores and pores and pores and skin down) and bake it for 45 minutes at 375 tiers F.

6) turn the portions over and allow it cook dinner dinner for five-10 mins in addition.

7) The crust turns into bubbly on the way to mean that the hen is cooked.

8) This recipe will offer you with three servings in widespread.

Nutritional data regular with serving:

Calories: 160kcal

Carbohydrates: 10g

Protein: 2g

Fat: 10g

Fiber: 1g

= = = = = = = = = = = = = = = = = = = =

Amish Pickled Eggs and Beets

What substances you could want:

1 cup cider vinegar

1 cup beet juice

15 ounce can small spherical beets

6 tough boiled eggs

1 teaspoon salt

half of of cup brown sugar

Directions:

1) First of all boil vinegar, beet juice, salt and brown sugar.

2) Now allow this combination to quiet down after which pour it on eggs and beets. After this vicinity it within the refrigerator for a night.

three) You can reduce eggs in to small portions earlier than servings them.

four) This recipe will come up with 6 servings in trendy.

Nutritional information in step with serving:

Calories: 180kcal

Carbohydrates: 26g

Protein: 8g

Fat: 10g

Fiber: 2g

= = = = = = = = = = = = = = = = = = = =

Amish Sugar Cookies

What materials you may want:

1 teaspoon baking soda

1 teaspoon vanilla

1 teaspoon cream of tartar

four half cups flour

1 cup cooking oil

2 eggs

1 cup butter

1 cup granulated sugar

1 cup powdered sugar

Directions:

1) Combine the following additives; sugar, powdered sugar, butter and cooking oil. Add in eggs and mix it nicely.

2) Further add in flour, cream of tartar, vanilla and baking soda. Stir in all the factors nicely.

3) Take a cookie sheet and drop some of the dough balls on it.

4) In a bowl, vicinity some granulated sugar and dip the lowest of a cup in it.

5) Flatten the dough with the help of the sugared backside of that glass at vicinity in oven to bake at 375 degrees.

6) Appropriate time to bake is 10-12 minutes or till you spot the cookies accumulate a colour of mild brown.

7) This recipe will provide you with 12 servings in normal.

Nutritional statistics in step with serving:

Calories: 190kcal

Carbohydrates: 20g

Protein: 2g

Fat: 10g

Fiber: 0g

====================

Amish Turnips

What factors you can need:

2/three cup breadcrumbs

salt and pepper

1 egg

1 cup milk

2 tablespoons brown sugar

1 tablespoon butter

2 cups cooked turnips

Directions:

1) First of all cook dinner turnips unless they will be mild. After cooking drain turnips and then mash them.

2) Add half cup bread crumbs in mashed turnip and placed all distinctive ingredients in it.

three) Mix a majority of these very well to make a mixture and pour it in a greasy baking dish.

four) Add very last bread crumbs on top of it and pour melted butter on it.

5) Now area this dish within the oven for baking.

6) Bake it on 375 diploma F 45 to 50 minutes.

7) Serve and revel in.

8) This recipe will provide you with 5 servings in total.

Nutritional information in line with serving:

Calories: 150kcal

Carbohydrates: 21g

Protein: 6g

Fat: 6g

Fiber: 2g

= = = = = = = = = = = = = = = = = = = =

Amish Soft Honey Whole Wheat Bread

What components you can need:

3 cups warmth water

2 tablespoons yeast

1 teaspoon sugar

11 -12 cups entire wheat flour

2 tablespoons salt

three/4 cup Crisco

3/4 cup honey

three eggs

Directions:

1) In a bowl, combine yeast with warmth water and sugar and leave for 10 mins to permit it to get foamy.

2) In the period in-between, location 3 eggs (with shell) in a bowl containing warm water. Add in flour, salt and gluten in the bowl.

3) Add inside the yeast aggregate and stir perfectly. Further add honey, eggs and Crisco and mix well till they will be combined and preserve scraping off the substances from the rims. An egg beater is appropriate for this.

four) Add in more flour and knead it flawlessly until it's smooth. Let it rest in a warm region until the scale of the dough is doubled.

five)   Divide in three identical loaves and leave it in a heat region all yet again, permitting it to chill (for an hour) Bake for 30-35 mins s regular bread is baked at 375 levels F.

6)   Serve and Enjoy!

7)   This recipe will offer you with 25 servings in popular.

Nutritional information consistent with serving:

Calories: 110kcal

Carbohydrates: 20g

Protein: 4g

Fat: 4g

Fiber: 3g

= = = = = = = = = = = = = = = = = = = =

Amish Dip

What elements you can want:

eight oz.. Cream cheese

half of cup mayonnaise

6 1/2 ounce can tuna

1/2 of of cup olive, pitted, chopped

half of of cup almonds chopped

black pepper

2 tablespoons lemon juice

Directions:

1)   First of all take a mixing bowl and upload all substances in it. Now mixture all factors very well, in this manner you could make a selection.

2)   Now you could serve it on heavy bread or you can make sandwiches of it.

3)   Serve and experience.

Nutritional statistics in keeping with serving:

Calories: 200kcal

Carbohydrates: 10g

Protein: 7g

Fat: 20g

Fiber: 1g

= = = = = = = = = = = = = = = = = = = =

Amish Blueberry Cake

What substances you'll want:

1/2 cup butter

1 cup sugar

1 cup blueberries

2 eggs

1 cup milk

3 teaspoons baking powder

half of of teaspoon salt

2 cups flour

Directions:

1) Take a mixing bowl and add all factors in it one after the alternative. Now mix all factors very well and make a batter.

2) Take a 9x13 period baking pan and pour batter in it.

3) Place this pan in oven for baking and bake it at 325 diploma F for 45 mins.

4) This recipe will offer you with 6 servings in elegant.

Nutritional information consistent with serving:

Calories: 480kcal

Carbohydrates: 60g

Protein: 10g

Fat: 20g

Fiber: 2g

= = = = = = = = = = = = = = = = = = = =

Amish Cream Pie

What components you could need:

2 half cups half of and half of of

1/4 teaspoon salt

1/four cup corn starch

3/4 cup sugar

half of cup butter

1/four cup packed brown sugar

1 teaspoon vanilla

1 9-inch baked pie crust

Directions:

1)   Mix in sugar, cornstarch and salt in a medium sized saucepan. Pour inside the half of and half of of of or cream and whisk it.

2)   Let it put together dinner over medium flame till the mixture becomes bubbly and thick. When it's performed, cast off from flame.

3)   Add in butter, brown sugar and vanilla and stir until the butter melts in properly. Take a pie shell (baked) and pour inside the mixture and dust cinnamon on it slightly.

4)   Bake the pie within the oven for spherical half of-hour and at 325 levels F. The middle of the pie will now not set so do now not exceed the baking time.

five)   Let the pie cool down for an hour on the cord rack and take a seat again it for three-6 hours earlier than serving.

6) If you want to shop it for prolonged time frame; keep it included.

7) This recipe will offer you with 8 servings in usual.

Nutritional data consistent with serving:

Calories: 400kcal

Carbohydrates: 41g

Protein: 4g

Fat: 24g

Fiber: 1g

= = = = = = = = = = = = = = = = = = = =

Amish Baked Macaroni and Cheese

What components you could need:

salt and pepper

breadcrumbs

8 ounces velveeta cheese

2 half of of cups milk

2 teaspoons salt

2 cups elbow macaroni

Directions:

1) First of all prepare dinner macaroni. After draining macaroni upload it in a casserole dish.

2) Now add cheese, milk, salt and pepper in casserole dish and blend all in additives thoroughly.

three) Sprinkle breadcrumbs on pinnacle of it.

4) Place casserole dish within the oven for baking way.

5) Bake it in oven at 325 degrees F for half-hour.

6) This recipe will provide you with four servings in general.

Nutritional facts in line with serving:

Calories: 460kcal

Carbohydrates: 51g

Protein: 21g

Fat: 19g

Fiber: 1.5g

= = = = = = = = = = = = = = = = = = = =

Lemon Poppy Seed Amish Friendship Bread

What factors you can want:

2 cups all purpose flour

1/2 of cup vegetable oil

1 cup amish starter

2 teaspoons vanilla extract

1/2 of cup applesauce

half of of cup milk

2 eggs

2 (3 ounce) programs right away lemon pudding mixture

1/eight cup poppy seed

1/2 teaspoon floor cinnamon

half of teaspoon baking soda

half of teaspoon salt

1 1/2 teaspoons baking powder

1 cup white sugar

Directions:

1) Take a large-sized bowl and mix in the following factors; flour, sugar, baking powder, poppy seeds, baking soda, cinnamon and lemon pudding combination. Create a nicely in the middle of the bowl.

2) Take every different bowl and blend within the Amish starter, eggs, milk, apple sauce, vanilla and vegetable oil.

three) Add this aggregate to the dry one and mix it well until the substances are blended. Grease 2 loaf pans and pour inside the aggregate in it.

four) Bake the combination for an hour at 325 levels F and allow cooling for as a minimum 10 mins at the wire rack.

five) Once it's chilled, cast off from the loaf pan.

6) This recipe will provide you with 24 servings in wellknown.

Nutritional records according to serving:

Calories: 150kcal

Carbohydrates: 24g

Protein: 2g

Fat: 6g

Fiber: zero.5g

= = = = = = = = = = = = = = = = = = = =

Amish-Style French Toast--Breakfast

What materials you may need:

1 cup milk

4 eggs

three/four teaspoon cinnamon

1/four teaspoon nutmeg

1/2 of teaspoon vanilla

1/4 teaspoon salt

1 sprint pepper

four -6 quantities bread

Directions:

1)	Take a mixing bowl and blend all components in it besides bread.

2) Now dip bread in this organized mixture.

3) Place a frying pan on range and heat it up.

four) Now vicinity bread within the heat frying pan and fry bread. Make bread brown from each factors.

5) This recipe will come up with 4 servings in widespread.

Nutritional records consistent with serving:

Calories: 138kcal

Carbohydrates: 7g

Protein: 9g

Fat: 9g

Fiber: zero.5g

= = = = = = = = = = = = = = = = = = =

Amish Rhubarb Pie

1 (nine inch) pie shells

4 cups rhubarb sliced 1 inch thick

1 cup sugar

four tablespoons all purpose flour

half teaspoon lemon juice

1 teaspoon salt

CRUMB TOPPING

1 cup all reason flour

1 dash salt

1/2 of of cup sugar

1/four cup softened butter

Directions:

1) Heat the oven in advance at 425 levels F.

2) Combine together the subsequent components; rhubarb, sugar, flour, lemon and salt. Pour this combination into baked pie shell and vicinity in oven. Bake for 30 minutes.

three) For the topping; Mix big crumbs with arms till they create sprinkle crumbs at the top.

4) Bake similarly for 15 mins just so the crumbs turn brown and the pie is bubbly. Let it cool.

five) This recipe will offer you with eight servings in widespread.

Nutritional facts in step with serving:

Calories: 150kcal

Carbohydrates: 17g

Protein: 4g

Fat: 4g

Fiber: 3g

= = = = = = = = = = = = = = = = = = = =

Amish Peanut Butter

What components you can need:

1 cup slight corn syrup

1/4 cup marshmallow cream

half of cup creamy peanut butter

Directions:

1) This is one of the simplest recipe within the e-book. Take a mixing bowl and mix all additives in this bowl. Now keep this amish peanut butter in fridge. You can use it as a selection. This recipe will come up with

almost 500 g of butter. Nutritional records beneath are for 500 g of butter.

Nutritional information in keeping with serving:

Calories: 1200kcal

Carbohydrates: 227g

Protein: 21g

Fat: 43g

Fiber: 5g

= = = = = = = = = = = = = = = = = = = =

Amish Brownies

What additives you could need:

4 ozBaking chocolate squares

2 cups chopped nuts

1 cup flour

1 sprint salt

2 tablespoons vanilla

four huge eggs

2 cups sugar

1 cup softened butter

Directions:

1) Take saucepan and melt chocolate and butter in it over medium warm temperature.

2) Remove saucepan from stove and now mixture all special substances in it and mix them nicely.

3) Take a 9x13 size pan and make it greasy with cooking spray. Now pour organized aggregate in the pan and area it in oven for baking.

4) Bake it in oven for 20 minutes at 350 stages F.

five) Serve and experience.

Nutritional facts consistent with serving:

Calories: 300kcal

Carbohydrates: 22g

Protein: 7g

Fat: 27g

Fiber: 4g

==========================

Amish Oats

What components you may need:

1 half of cups short cooking oats

1/four cup brown sugar

half of cup milk

3/4 teaspoon salt

1 teaspoon vanilla extract

1 teaspoon baking powder

1 egg

1/four cup melted butter

Directions:

1) In a blending bowl combo all additives to make a combination. Take a baking pan of any length and make it greasy. Now unfold aggregate in the baking pan. Place baking pan inside the oven for baking manner. Bake it for 20 to 1/2-hour at 350 degrees F. Serve it and experience. This recipe will give you four servings in traditional.

Nutritional records consistent with serving:

Calories: 310kcal

Carbohydrates: 35g

Protein: 8g

Fat: 17g

Fiber: 3g

= = = = = = = = = = = = = = = = = = = =

Amish Caramel Pudding

What factors you'll want:

4 tablespoons butter

four cups milk

1 cup brown sugar

1/four teaspoon salt

2/three cup flour

2 teaspoons vanilla

Directions:

1)   Preheat a pan and melt butter in it. Now Add milk in it and bowl it. After this add sugar,

salt and flour within the milk and put together dinner until it end up a thick combination.

2) Remove pan from stove and add vanilla in it.

three) Now allow it to cool down and it is prepared to serve.

4) This recipe will give you 4 servings in regular.

Nutritional records in line with serving:

Calories: 310kcal

Carbohydrates: 35g

Protein: 8g

Fat: 17g

Fiber: 3g

= = = = = = = = = = = = = = = = = = = =

Amish Boiled Cookies

What substances you can want:

3 tablespoons unsweetened cocoa

half of of of cup reduced-fats peanut butter

2 cups sugar

half of cup low fats milk

half of cup moderate butter

1 teaspoon vanilla

1/4 teaspoon salt

three cups brief cooking oats

1/2 of cup chopped pecans

Directions:

1) Over medium flame, blend together butter, milk, sugar and cocoa in a small saucepan. Let them come to a boil and put together dinner dinner further for 60 seconds.

2) Remove the pan from flame and upload in peanut butter, vanilla and salt. Mix well. Stir in oats and pecans.

three) With the help of a small cookie scoop (you could use a teaspoon as well), hunch the combination at once to the waxed paper.

four) Leave the cookies for an hour; this may permit them to face after which tore them in a closed (air tight) subject.

5) This recipe will provide you with 24 servings in ordinary.

Nutritional records in line with serving:

Calories: 80kcal

Carbohydrates: 13g

Protein: 2g

Fat: 3g

Fiber: 1g

= = = = = = = = = = = = = = = = = = =

Amish Pineapple Delight

What components you could want:

6 ounces. Orange gelatin

three oz. Lemon gelatin

10 ouncespineapple chew

8 ouncescool whip

6 oz.. Cherries tired

10 oz... Miniature marshmallows

Directions:

1) In separate bowls blend each gelatins in step with their package deal deal deal instructions.

2) Place every bowls in the fridge sincerely so they come to be set.

three) Cut gelatin after which integrate them with tired stop result. Chill it in fridge and then it is ready to serve.

four) This recipe will offer you with 4 servings in accepted.

Nutritional records in line with serving:

Calories: 410kcal

Carbohydrates: 50g

Protein: 8g

Fat: 14g

Fiber: 3g

= = = = = = = = = = = = = = = = = = = =

Amish Oatmeal Whoopie Pie Cookies

What elements you could need:

2 cups slight brown sugar

3/4 cup butter

2 massive eggs

1/2 teaspoon salt

2 cups flour

2 cups brief cooking oatmeal

1 teaspoon baking powder

1 teaspoon ground cinnamon

2 teaspoons baking soda

3 teaspoons boiling water

FILLING

1 egg white

1/four cup vegetable shortening

2 cups powdered sugar

2 tablespoons milk

1 tablespoon vanilla

Directions:

1) To create the oatmeal cookie mixture; take cream butter, sugar and eggs. Sieve flour, salt and baking powder and mix into the

cream mixture. Mix in cinnamon and oatmeal. Stir it gently.

2)   On the opportunity hand; in heat water, upload soda and it to the batter and blend well to unite the elements.

3)   Grease a cookie sheet and drop the mixture on it with the assist of a teaspoon. Bake in oven, for 15-19 mins at 325 ranges F.

four)   For the filling; combo collectively egg white, vanilla, milk and 1 cup of powdered sugar. Beat them well so they shape a cream and upload within the last materials.

five)   Beat constantly for a similarly 3 minutes.

6)   Add the filling among cookies and wrap every whoopee pie cookie in plastic wrap.

7)   This recipe will offer you with 15 servings in widespread.

Nutritional facts consistent with serving:

Calories: 250kcal

Carbohydrates: 40g

Protein: 3g

Fat: 9g

Fiber: 1g

= = = = = = = = = = = = = = = = = = = =

Amish Cinnamon Bread

What additives you may need:

1 cup milk

1 cup flour

1 cup sugar

On Day 6 upload

1 cup milk

1 cup flour

1 cup sugar

On Day 10 add

1 cup milk

1 cup flour

1 cup sugar

1 cup vegetable oil

half of cup milk

3 eggs

1 teaspoon vanilla

2 cup flour

1 cup sugar

2 teaspoons cinnamon

1 1/2 of teaspoons baking powder

1/2 teaspoon salt

1 (6 ounce) container vanilla right now pudding mixture

half teaspoon baking soda

1 cup nuts (non-obligatory)

half of cup raisins

Directions:

1) Day 1: Combine 1 cup milk, 1 cup sugar and 1 cup flour in a ziplock bag and mush the factors to combine them well with every exceptional.

2) Day 2-five: Mush the bag daily at least times.

3) Day 6: adjoin 1 cup milk, 1 cup sugar and 1 cup flour within the bag and break it once more so it is combined nicely.

four) Day 7-9: Remove air and then mush it all over again on times basis every day.

five) Day 10: Pour out the components of the ziplock bag in a big bowl. Mix in 1 cup milk, 1 cup sugar and 1 cup flour and blend to mix properly.

6) Now degree four starters and you could additionally keep starters in freezer for destiny use. In the bowl, combo in eggs, milk, oil and vanilla.

7) Now add the leftover elements and stir well to mix all materials. If you need to, then add in nuts and raisins and fold them in.

eight) Now take loaf pans and spray them with cooking spray. Dust it nicely sugar and cinnamon.

9) Empty the batter into the loaf pans similarly and bake for one hour minimum or until its absolutely prepared at 325 tiers F.

10) If you're making cakes out of this aggregate, bake for best 25 minutes.

eleven) This recipe will provide you with 25 servings in stylish.

Nutritional records in step with serving:

Calories: 200kcal

Carbohydrates: 19g

Protein: 3g

Fat: 7g

Fiber: 1g

= = = = = = = = = = = = = = = = = = =

Amish Sticky Buns

What components you can want:

2 tablespoons yeast

1 tablespoon sugar

1 cup milk

1 cup water

6 tablespoons butter

half of cup sugar

1 teaspoon salt

7 cups flour

three beaten eggs

Syrup

3 cups brown sugar

three/four cup butter

6 tablespoons Karo syrup Topping

Brown sugar

Directions:

1) Mix yeast in heat water evenly. Blister a few milk and add in butter, sugar and salt. Let it cool until its lukewarm and then add cups of flour.

2) Further add eggs and yeast and stir within the leftover flour as properly. Knead it gently and go away it to upward push at least to double of its size.

3) In the interim, boil the syrup elements for at least 2 mins. Take 6 eight inch rectangular pans and in addition pour within the syrup mixture in them for my part.

4) Meanwhile, the dough may be doubled or wait until it is doubled. Once it's finished, divide the dough into factors.

5) Roll each the factors one after the alternative proper right right into a 12x18 inch rectangle on a flour dusted board or table. Dust a few brown sugar and cinnamon on top.

6) Roll every piece tightly and begin rolling from the vast facet.

7) Now, cut it into 1 inch slices and installation the slices on pinnacle of the syrup which you have poured into the pans in addition.

eight) Bake in oven for 15 mins best at 375 levels F.

9) This recipe will provide you with 25 servings in great.

Nutritional facts in step with serving:

Calories: 180kcal

Carbohydrates: 30g

Protein: 3g

Fat: 5g

Fiber: 1g

= = = = = = = = = = = = = = = = = = = =

Amish Biscuits

What components you'll need:

1 cup all motive flour

half of teaspoon baking soda

1/2 teaspoon salt

2 teaspoons baking powder

2 eggs

1 cup amish starter

1/4 cup vegetable oil

1/4 cup melted butter

Directions:

1) Mix in baking powder, salt, baking soda and flour in a large sized bowl.

2) Take some one-of-a-kind bowl and integrate the subsequent elements; eggs, Amish starter and oil. Mix it properly.

3) Insert the starter into the dry mixture and mix properly until the dough leaves the sides of the bowl. Lightly dust flour on a ground and flip out the dough on it.

four) Keep rolling the dough until it receives ½ inch thick. With the help of a 3 inch circle cutter, cut out biscuits from the dough.

5) Grease a cookie sheet and set up the biscuits on it. At the top of the biscuits, area some melted butter with a broom and cowl them.

6) Leave them for half-hour for letting them upward push. Once they upward thrust, bake for 15-20 minutes in preheated 350 levels oven.

7) This recipe will provide you with 24 servings in popular.

Nutritional information in step with serving:

Calories: 60kcal

Carbohydrates: 4g

Protein: 1g

Fat: 5g

Fiber: 1g

= = = = = = = = = = = = = = = = = = =

Amish Onion Patties

What factors you could need:

1 tablespoon cornmeal

1 tablespoon sugar

3/four cup flour

2 teaspoons baking powder

1 -2 teaspoon salt

3/4 cup milk

2 half of cups chopped onions

Directions:

1) Mix all of the dry materials together and pour in milk in them. Mix it properly until it paperwork an top notch and thick batter.

2) When finished, upload in onions and begin losing the batter with a spoon, in warm deep fats. Let them be for 3-four mins or when they get golden on one thing.

three) Change their issue and compress them for patties.

4) Fry the second one factor as properly until it is also golden (about 3-four mins another time) and drain out the excessive oil.

five) This recipe will offer you with four servings in standard.

Nutritional statistics consistent with serving:

Calories: 170kcal

Carbohydrates: 34g

Protein: 5g

Fat: 2g

Fiber: 2g

= = = = = = = = = = = = = = = = = = = =

Amish Noodles

What factors you will need:

2 tablespoons vegetable oil

6 tablespoons water

2 complete eggs

1 1/four teaspoons salt

2 cups bread flour

Directions:

1) In a bowl, location a few flour and create a well within the center. Stir within the closing elements and mix with the help of a fork until a ball forms.

2) Take the long-established ball out and place on a floor dusted with flour and knead it for about five mins.

3) Cover the dough with a towel and allow it to rest for at least 45 mins. After it has rested for the given time, lessen it down into quarters and roll out one fourth right into a rectangle 8x14 till it gets skinny as paper.

4) Flour every elements of it and located it sideways. Roll the last sections within the same way and stack them one over every other and permit them to relaxation for at least half of-hour.

5) Now, starting with the shortest element roll them up like a jelly roll and reduce them with a knife within the width you choice.

6) If they may be moist, dirt with a few flour. Now, unroll the circles and divide them.

7) Leave them for drying (it is able to take hours as well). Once it's completed, prepare dinner in broth for 5-7 mins.

eight) This recipe will provide you with eight servings in widespread.

Nutritional data consistent with serving:

Calories: 160kcal

Carbohydrates: 24g

Protein: 5g

Fat: 5g

Fiber: 1g

= = = = = = = = = = = = = = = = = = = =

Amish Cake

What substances you will need:

half of of cup butter

2 cups brown sugar

2 cups buttermilk

2 teaspoons baking soda

three cups flour

1 teaspoon vanilla essence

Topping

half cup chopped nuts

1 cup sugar

4 tablespoons milk

6 tablespoons easy butter

Directions:

1)   Heat the oven beforehand at 375 levels F. On the opportunity hand, take a 9x13 pan and dirt its bottom with flour.

2)   For cake: Mix in cream, butter and sugar except they are fluffy. When its fluffy, pour in buttermilk or sour milk and a couple of teaspoons of baking soda and mix.

3)   They batter want to be a chunk foamy. Now add in flour and blend it nicely until all the elements are combined together. In the give up, upload vanilla.

4) Empty the batter within the 9x13 pan and bake until your checking knife comes out clean (this will take approximately 25-half of-hour).

5) For topping: Blend the following elements in a small bowl; smooth butter, milk, brown sugar and nuts.

6) When the cake is accomplished and is warm temperature unfold the topping on it and placed all over again inside the oven. Bake it for a minute or until it becomes bubbly.

7) Take out from the oven and funky earlier than serving.

eight) This recipe will provide you with 12 servings in widespread.

Nutritional information in step with serving:

Calories: 400kcal

Carbohydrates: 64g

Protein: 7g

Fat: 15g

Fiber: 2g

= = = = = = = = = = = = = = = = = = =

Amish Potato Rolls

What substances you'll want:

5 teaspoons yeast

2 cups water

eight -nine cups bread flour

3/4 cup Crisco

2 cups mashed potatoes

1 tablespoon salt

five eggs

1 cup sugar

Directions:

1) Place water for your mixer and spray yeast in it. Let the yeast prompt after which add sugar to it. Mix!

2) Now add in shortening, eggs, salt and potatoes. Add cups of flour one after the alternative, and stop on the eighth one. If you have any final flour, add it best to get a barely sticky feeling. The dough want to not be dry!

3) Grease a bowl and place the dough in it and cover up. Leave it in a warmth location so that it could rise (as a minimum double of its real length).

four) Measure ½ cup of flour and upload inside the bowl. Spray pan spray for your hands. Now break the dough and make rolls out of it. Roll a piece in flour to coat it.

five) Grease a pan and arrange them on it. Leave them to upward thrust until they're doubled. Bake in oven for 20-25 mins at 350 ranges F (preheated).

6) It should have a light brown color, so that you mentioned that it's finished. The prep time isn't always included in the upward push time as it varies.

7) This recipe will offer you with 18 servings in overall.

Nutritional facts consistent with serving:

Calories: 180kcal

Carbohydrates: 29g

Protein: 4g

Fat: 5g

Fiber: 1g

Amish White Bread

What additives you may need:

2 1/2 tablespoons shortening

1/four ounce dry yeast

1/2 cup water

1/three cup sugar

6 -7 cups all-reason flour or 6 -7 cups bread flour

1/eight-1/4 cup butter

2 teaspoons salt

2 cups water

Directions:

1) Dissolve yeast in 1/2 of cup of warm water. In a great bowl, combine sugar, salt, cups of water and shortening. Stir in the yeast combos.

2) Steadily encompass flour to make it easy dough.

3) Turn at once to floured surface and knead till glossy. Spot in a greased bowl after which cover it and permit it to rise for about 2 hours.

four) Punch down and divide in to two factors and make loaves. Spot in greased 9 into 5 inches loaf pans and prick tops with the fork.

5) Let it upward push right until it is higher than the pans (about hrs).

6) Bake it at 375 ranges for twenty five to thirty minutes. Let it's cooled for ten mins. Rub the butter everywhere in the tops of the loaves.

7) Keep the pans on element's right till loosened.

8) Remove the bread from the pans and allow them to be cooled truely on the racks.

9) Serve and enjoy Amish White Bread!!

10) This Original recipe makes 24 servings in common.

Nutritional statistics in line with serving:

Serving period: 62g

Calories: 147kcal

Carbohydrates: 27g

Protein: 4g

Fat: 3g

Fiber: zero.9g

Amish Baked Oatmeal

What ingredients you may want:

1 cup milk

2 tablespoons milk

3 cups oatmeal (ordinary or short)

1 1/2 teaspoons vanilla

1 teaspoon nutmeg or 1 teaspoon cinnamon

1/four teaspoon salt

1/three cup butter

2 large eggs

three/four cup brown sugar

1 1/2 teaspoons baking powder

Directions:

1) Turn for your oven and preheat that to 350 degrees. Grease a thirteen x 9 x baking pan.

2) Combine all the components alongside every exclusive. Unfold on nicely organized baking pan.

three) Bake it for twenty 5-to- thirty minutes or until in the end the rims are golden browned. Promptly spoon that right into a bowl.

4) Top with the nice and relaxed milk, a few sparkling fruit or brown sugar in case you need to.

5) Serve and enjoy Amish Baked Oatmeal!!

6) This Original recipe makes 6 servings in everyday.

Nutritional records in keeping with serving:

Serving length: 145g

Calories: 407kcal

Carbohydrates: 57g

Protein: 9g

Fat: 16g

Fiber: 5g

Amish Soft Pretzels

What factors you may need:

1/four cup brown sugar

2 cups occident flour (bread flour)

2 cups flour

1 1/4 cups water

1 tablespoon yeast

Dipping solution

candy creamy butter

1/2 cup baking soda, into

three cups warm water

Directions:

1)   Dissolve the yeast in to warm temperature consuming water. Add a few sugar, then flour & combination very well- however do no longer 'knead' as this toughens up the dough. (Combine genuinely proper up till combined well)

2)   Let it upward thrust proper until doubled, at the least twenty mins.

3)   Now reduce it in to Long Ropes. Shape it into pretzel shapes, and then dip it into prepared dipping answer.

4)   Put on nicely-greased cookie sheet and sprinkle it with pretzel salt.

five)   Bake it at "500-550°F" for four-to- six mins proper up until golden browned. Dip the front of pretzel in to the melted butter.

6)   Variation: encompass one t vanilla to the prepared dough. Taste variations. Cinnamon/sugar- miss salt& dip into cinnamon sugar proper after the front has been covered with the butter.

7) Sour cream & onion- sincerely after dipping the the front of pretzel into the butter.

8) Sprinkle it with the bitter creams & onions powder Garlic- very same as sour creams & onions but hire garlic powder.

nine) Sesame or the poppy seed--Ahead of baking, quick after dipping into organized dipping answer, dip pretzel the the the front-down in to seeds, and then bake it.

10) Salt is surely non-compulsory with this recipe.

11) Serve and enjoy Amish Soft Pretzels!!

12) This Original recipe makes 10 servings in wellknown.

Nutritional facts in keeping with serving:

Serving length: 170g

Calories: 210kcal

Carbohydrates: 36g

Protein: 5g

Fat: 2g

Fiber: 2g

Amish Turnips

What materials you may need:

1 tablespoon margarine

2 tablespoons brown sugar

1 cup milk

1 egg

salt and pepper

2 cups cooked turnips

2/3 cup breadcrumbs

Directions:

1)   Prepare dinner turnips until in the long run tendered.

2)   Drain, mash and then encompass half of of a cup bread crumbs, saving and reserving rest for the top.

three) Break in eggs, sugar, milk, salt and pepper to the taste. Blend collectively; pour it in to the greased baking dish.

four) Dot it with the butter and rest of the crumbs.

five) Bake it for forty five mins at "375F" Degrees.

6) Serve and experience Amish Turnips!!

7) This Original recipe makes 5 servings in usual.

Nutritional records in step with serving:

Serving length: 130g

Calories: 160kcal

Carbohydrates: 22g

Protein: 6g

Fat: 6g

Fiber: 2g

Amish Meatloaf Recipe

What factors you could want:

3/4 cup ketchup

2 teaspoons garlic salt

1/4-1/2 teaspoon pepper (to taste)

2 lbs extra lean floor red meat

1 3/four cups Ritz crackers, overwhelmed

1 small onion, chopped finely

2 eggs, barely overwhelmed

FOR SAUCE

1/2 teaspoon dry mustard

2 tablespoons dark brown sugar

1/8-1/four teaspoon pepper (to flavor)

1/2 cup ketchup

1/4 teaspoon salt

Directions:

1)   Mix up the primary seven additives thoroughly collectively and then % them in to a "loaf pan".

2) Meanwhile, mix up the sauces components all collectively.

3) When the sixty mins are up, pour up and clean up the sauces on to meatloaf after which prepare dinner it for fifteen to twenty minutes greater.

four) Sometimes i add half of of teaspoon of the garlic salt surely as opposed to salt to sauce aggregate and that is without a doubt delicious! Choice is yours!

five) Serve and enjoy Amish Meatloaf Recipe!!

6) This Original recipe makes 4 servings in ordinary.

Nutritional facts in keeping with serving:

Serving length: 255g

Calories: 600kcal

Carbohydrates: 45g

Protein: 55g

Fat: 22g

Fiber: 2g

Amish Noodles

What substances you can need:

2 (14 ounce) cans chicken broth

12 oz. Egg noodles

2 tablespoons butter

1 bird bouillon dice

Directions:

1) Take a huge pan, and brown butter in it.

2) Add the bouillon dice, and broth, and then bring it to a boil.

three) Add the noodles, and then convey it to a boil again, cowl it and flip off the warmth. (Just depart the pot over identical burner).

4) Allow it to face for approximately thirty minutes, Stir it for 2 or 3 instances.

5) Serve and enjoy Amish Noodles!!

6) This Original recipe makes four servings in trendy.

Nutritional statistics in line with serving:

Serving length: 255g

Calories: 600kcal

Carbohydrates: 45g

Protein: 55g

Fat: 22g

Fiber: 2g

Amish Apple Crisp

What components you will need:

1/three cup sugar

1 teaspoon cinnamon

5 -6 apples, peeled and sliced

TOPPING

1 unbeaten egg

1/2 teaspoon cinnamon

1/3 cup butter, melted

1 cup flour

1/2 cup sugar

1 teaspoon baking powder

1/2 teaspoon salt

Directions:

1) Put the apple mixture in a deep dish pie pan. Sprinkle it with cinnamon, and sugar.

2) Mix up the topping substances, Apart from the butter, and cinnamon, with a fork proper till properly blended.

3) Sprinkle topping on the pinnacle of apples.

4) Drizzle the melted butter on the top of sprinkled topping. Sprinkle it with cinnamon.

5) Bake it at "375°F" Degrees for 40 mins.

6) Serve heat and experience Amish Apple Crisp!!

7) This Original recipe makes 6 servings in popular.

Nutritional data in line with serving:

Serving size: 200g

Calories: 420kcal

Carbohydrates: 62g

Protein: 17g

Fat: 11g

Fiber: 3g

Amish Dip

What materials you may want:

1/2 cup walnuts or 1/2 cup almonds, chopped

2 tablespoons lemon juice

black pepper

8 oz.. Cream cheese

1/2 cup mayonnaise

1 (6 1/2 of ounce) can tuna

1/2 cup olive, pitted, chopped

Directions:

1) Mix all factors in a bowl. You can add more or lots an awful lot much less mayonnaise and it's miles up on your taste.

2) Serve it as a range with heavy bread.

3) Serve and experience.

4) This Original recipe makes three cups in ordinary.

Nutritional information in step with serving:

Serving length: 56g

Calories: 50kcal

Carbohydrates: 8g

Protein: 13g

Fat: 18g

Fiber: 2g

Amish Friendship Bread And Starter

What materials you may want:

Starter

3 cups sugar, divided

3 cups milk, divided

3 cups flour, divided

Bread

1 cup chopped nuts

1 tablespoon cinnamon, combined with

1/2 cup sugar

1/2 teaspoon salt

1/2 teaspoon baking soda

1 (five 1/8 ounce) region without delay vanilla pudding

1 cup sugar

1 1/2 teaspoons baking powder

2 teaspoons cinnamon

1 cup oil

1/2 cup milk

three entire eggs

1 teaspoon vanilla extract

2 cups flour

Directions:

1) Put one cup each flour, milk and sugar in a big plastic or a tumbler bowl.

2) Cover it gently with the plastic wrapper after which set it at the counter at everyday room temperature.

3) Stir it with the help of a wood spoon every day for seventeen days.

four) When it's the day eighteen simply do nothing.

five) When it's the times nineteen, twenty, and twenty one, stir it.

6) When it's the day twenty , add one cup of sugar, one cup of milk, and one cup of flour, after which stir it once more.

7) When it's the instances twenty 3, twenty four, twenty 5, and twenty six do stir it.

8) When it's the day Twenty seven, add one cup of milk, one cup of flour, and one cup of sugar and then stir.

nine) Now it is ready to be utilized in making of the bread.

10) Give away the 2 cups of starter to the 2 buddies of yours, just use one very last cup in making of the bread, and actually preserve one cup to keep "starter going". As you "offer away" one cup of the starter on your buddy, deliver the ones suggestions handiest for "retaining it going"

11) Remember now not to refrigerate; not to use a steel spoon or a steel bowl; not to cover it tightly, just cover it loosely with a plastic wrap.

12) It's AMISH BREAD of FRIENDSHIP: Mix the vanilla, eggs and oil with starter aggregate.

13) Take a separate bowl, and mix nuts, vanilla pudding mixture, baking soda, salt, cinnamon, baking powder, sugar and flour.

14) Add to the liquid combo after which stir it very well.

15) Pour it into 2 huge "properly-greased 9 x Five inch" loaf pans, or certainly one "Bundt pan", this is been sprinkled with the combination of flour, sugar and cinnamon.

sixteen) Sprinkle some more sugar, and cinnamon onto the top of unbaked loaves (or the cake). Bake it at "325F" levels for sixty minutes or honestly till it's carried out.

17) This Original recipe makes 15 servings in general.

Nutritional statistics steady with serving:

Serving length: 156g

Calories: 305kcal

Carbohydrates: 50g

Protein: 4g

Fat: 10g

Fiber: 2g

Amish Macaroni & Cheese

What materials you may need:

sixteen ozwater

sixteen oz. Shredded cheddar cheese

1 (16 ounce) difficulty cottage cheese

16 ozOf uncooked elbow macaroni

Directions:

1) Take a 9 x 13 duration baking pan and upload cottage cheese in it.

2) Now upload all remaining materials and blend them properly.

three) Put this baking pan in oven and bake it at three hundred levels F for 60 mins. Do not neglect to check pan after every 1/2-hour because of the reality we do no longer need to overcook it.

4) Serve and experience.

5) This Original recipe makes 15 servings in regular.

Nutritional facts consistent with serving:

Serving length: 156g

Calories: 341kcal

Carbohydrates: 31g

Protein: 20g

Fat: 15g

Fiber: 2g

Amish Pot Roast

What substances you could need:

soy sauce, as desired

2 bay leaves, crumbled

1 clove garlic, finely minced

1/2 teaspoon dried oregano

three lbs swiss steak, trimmed of fats

1 tablespoon vegetable oil

1/four cup soy sauce

1 cup coffee

2 onions, sliced

Directions:

1)   Turn to your oven and preheat it to "300F" tiers.

2)   Remember not to pound or flour up the beef. Heat some oil in a huge sized skillet over

a excessive temperature, and then sear the pork at the each components.

three) Meanwhile, take a big sized "roasting pan", and combine the one of the sliced onions, oregano, garlic, bay leaves, espresso and soy sauce.

four) Now Transfer all of the red meat browned to the "roasting pan".

five) Top it with the 2d sliced onion.

6) Cover it after which bake it for three and a half of of of to 4 hours, basting it every single hour with the pan juice.

7) If liquid starts offevolved to "boil away", add one extra cup espresso after which a sprint of the soy sauce.

eight) May be you may be needing to copy this way; keep in mind that there ought to be virtually quite a chunk of the liquid.

nine) Cut off the meat into the thin slices and then serve it with the pan juices.

10) Serve and experience.

11) This Original recipe makes 6 servings in regular.

Nutritional facts in keeping with serving:

Serving length: 318g

Calories: 337kcal

Carbohydrates: 5g

Protein: 52g

Fat: 11g

Fiber: 1g

Amish Baked Chicken

What components you could want:

1/4 teaspoon dry mustard

3 teaspoons salt

1 split broiler chickens

1/four lb butter

1/2 cup flour

2 teaspoons paprika

1 teaspoon pepper

Directions:

1) Mix up the dried substances nicely using the plastic bag, after which use this mixture to coat the hen portions.

2) Take a "cake pan", and soften a few butter in it.

three) Put chook quantities into the cake pan, however recollect now not to crowd up them.

4) Bake chicken portions at "350F" stages for one and a 1/2 of to 2 hours or sincerely till it's completed.

five) Serve and revel in.

6) This Original recipe makes four servings in traditional.

Nutritional information consistent with serving:

Serving length: 280g

Calories: 760kcal

Carbohydrates: 13g

Protein: 45g

Fat: 58g

Fiber: 1g

Amish Pickled Eggs And Beets

What substances you may want:

1 teaspoon salt

6 tough-boiled eggs, shelled

1 (15 ounce) cansmall spherical beets

1 cup cider vinegar

1 cup beet juice (upload water, if crucial, to make 1 cup)

1/2 cup brown sugar

Directions:

1) First of all boil beet juice, salt, vinegar and brown sugar.

2) Now allow it to settle down after which upload it over eggs and beets.

3) Serve eggs after lowering them into small portions.

4) This Original recipe makes 6 servings in usual.

Nutritional facts consistent with serving:

Serving period: 180g

Calories: 187kcal

Carbohydrates: 26g

Protein: 8g

Fat: 6g

Fiber: 2g

Dried Beef Gravy

What components you'll want:

3 tablespoons flour

three cups milk

1/4 lb dried red meat

2 tablespoons butter

Directions:

1) Melt the butter the use of a medium sized skillet.

2) Tear down the dry pork in-to small sized quantities and then stir' them in-to the melted butter.

three) Now Brown the pork slightly.

four) Stir that in the flour.

5) When the flour is truely dissolved into the butter, add the milk, and stir it regularly.

6) Cook it over the low warm temperature proper until the aggregate thickens itself.

7) This Original recipe makes 4 servings in average.

Nutritional statistics consistent with serving:

Serving duration: 224g

Calories: 232kcal

Carbohydrates: 14g

Protein: 16g

Fat: 13g

Fiber: 0.2g

Amish Beef Stew

What additives you can want:

6 potatoes, peeled and decrease into chunks

1/2 cup bloodless water

1/4 cup flour

2 -three lbs boneless red meat cubes

2 tablespoons shortening

1 massive onion, sliced

1 sprint allspice

1 dash clove

6 carrots, peeled and reduce into chunks

1 tablespoon Worcestershire sauce

1/2 teaspoon pepper

1 1/2 teaspoons paprika

four cups boiling water

1 tablespoon salt

1 tablespoon lemon juice

1 tablespoon sugar

Directions:

1) Melt the shortening at immoderate warmth the usage of a massive sized pot or a "Dutch oven".

2) Add the pork cubes in it and then brown them over a medium degree of heat, stir it occasionally, for approximately fifteen-to-twenty minutes.

three) Now upload the cloves, allspice, paprika, pepper, Worcestershire sauce, sugar, lemon juice, salt, boiling water and onions.

4) Simmer it; tightly cowl it, about Couple of hours, stir it every so often.

five) Now Add the vegetables and then simmer it for every different thirty minutes (on the equal time as covered), or certainly until tendered.

6) Note: if the lid isn't really tight over the pot, this may not have ok fluid left to cowl everything after including the greens.

7) In that case, add some extra water with a purpose to barely cowl the factors.

8) Mix the bloodless water and the flour all together and then combination it until smoothens.

nine) Push the pork and vegetables within the direction of the edges of pot and then upload the flour combination steadily, incorporating into the liquid.

10) When the gravy is thickened, fire up all of the components slowly that allows you to distribute the gravy uniformly.

eleven) Make it Simmer for some special 5 or ten mins, enjoy!

12) This Original recipe makes 6 servings in normal.

Nutritional facts normal with serving:

Serving size: 486g

Calories: 1291kcal

Carbohydrates: 53g

Protein: 19g

Fat: 113g

Fiber: 8g

Whole Wheat Bread

What elements you will need:

2 tablespoons salt

eleven -12 cups whole wheat flour

four tablespoons wheat gluten (non-obligatory)

three eggs

three⁄4 cup honey

3⁄4 cup Crisco (I use butter flavored)

three cups warmness water (a hundred and ten-one hundred fifteen ranges)

1 teaspoon sugar

2 tablespoons yeast

Directions:

1) Mix up the water with the yeast and the sugar and let it sit proper till foamy (for about ten mins).

2) Meanwhile, location the 3 eggs (in a shallow) the use of a bowl of warmth water (to carry eggs to the room temperature).

3) Put gluten, salt and flour in a bowl.

4) Pour over the yeast mixture and stir it until properly blended. Now add in the crisco, eggs and honey till properly blended, scrap the sides. (I use eggs beater for doing this).

five) Now upload a few greater "wheat flour" and knead it proper till smoothens.

6) Let it set in a warm region about sixty mins or really till doubled inside the period.

7) Divide that into three loaves. And Let that rise another time inside the warm temperature vicinity right until double in duration (approximately one and a half of hours).

8) Bake it similar to a ordinary bread ("I typically bake it about thirty five mins at "375F" or simply till the internal of bread is at

"190F" stages showing at electric powered powered powered thermometer").

nine) Serve and Enjoy!

10) This Original recipe makes 60 servings in preferred.

Nutritional statistics in keeping with serving:

Serving length: 44g

Calories: 115kcal

Carbohydrates: 20g

Protein: 4g

Fat: 4g

Fiber: 3g

Amish Crazy Quilt Pie

What additives you can want:

1/2 cup butter, room temperature

1/2 teaspoon salt

1 teaspoon vanilla extract

2 cups milk, can also moreover use lower fats

four huge eggs

1/2 cup all-motive flour

1 cup sweetened flaked coconut

1 cup granulated sugar

Directions:

1) Put all of the elements in-to a jug of a blender,

2) Turn blender on a medium degree of tempo after which count to ten. Pour this right into a 9 inches deep "dish pie" pan.

three) Meanwhile baking system is taking walks, flour will drop to transform the crust. The relaxation of the materials shape the fillings.

four) Bake it at "350*F" for 45 mins.

five) Serve and Enjoy!

6) This Original recipe makes 8 servings in popular.

Nutritional information in line with serving:

Serving period: 145g

Calories: 361kcal

Carbohydrates: 20g

Protein: 7g

Fat: 21g

Fiber: 0.7g

Amish Baked Apples

What components you can want:

1 teaspoon cinnamon

2 teaspoons butter, melted

1 cup water

8 -10 apples, cored, peeled

3/four cup white sugar

3/four cup brown sugar

1/2 cup flour

Directions:

1)   Put apples in a nicely-greased 9 x Thirteen inches baking dish.

2)   Mix up the rest of the substances all together at the same time as maintaining the given ORDER, inside the pan and then supply that to a boil.

3)   Make it Simmer, stir it proper until thickens.

4)   Pour the syrup over the apples and then bake that at "350°F" for Thirty five to forty minutes or proper until tendered.

5)   Serve and Enjoy!

6)   This Original recipe makes 8 servings in overall.

Nutritional statistics steady with serving:

Serving duration: 260g

Calories: 260kcal

Carbohydrates: 20g

Protein: 2g

Fat: 2g

Fiber: 0.6g

www.ingramcontent.com/pod-product-compliance
Lightning Source LLC
Chambersburg PA
CBHW050400120526
44590CB00015B/1763